KANT'S PHILOSOPHY
OF RELIGION

Oxford University Press

London   Edinburgh   Glasgow   Copenhagen
New York   Toronto   Melbourne   Cape Town
Bombay   Calcutta   Madras   Shanghai
Humphrey Milford Publisher to the UNIVERSITY

KANT'S PHILOSOPHY OF RELIGION

By

CLEMENT C. J. WEBB

Oriel Professor of Philosophy of the
Christian Religion in the
University of Oxford

OXFORD

At the Clarendon Press

1926

Printed in England
At the OXFORD UNIVERSITY PRESS
By John Johnson
Printer to the University

PREFACE

THE following chapters embody the substance of a course of lectures delivered at Oxford in the Michaelmas Term of 1924, the year in which was celebrated the bicentenary of Kant's birth. In them I have endeavoured to give a connected view of Kant's contributions to the Philosophy of Religion from the *Allgemeine Naturgeschichte* of 1755 to the fragments which pass under the name of the *Opus Postumum*, written in the last years of his life nearly half a century later, and now available for study in Professor Adickes's edition of 1920. The references in the foot-notes are to Hartenstein's edition of the *Werke*, 1867–8, or, in the case of the *Opus Postumum*, to that of Professor Adickes already mentioned; but an Index of the passages quoted or discussed in the course of the book, arranged according to the chronological order of Kant's writings, will enable the reader to find the corresponding places in the new Berlin edition.

Oxford, 1926.

CONTENTS

I

INTRODUCTORY

In the year 1924 was celebrated the bicentenary of Kant's birth at Königsberg on 22nd April 1724, and it seemed to me that a Professor of the Philosophy of the Christian Religion might appropriately recognize the fact by devoting a term's course of lectures to the contribution made by this great man to the special subject of his chair. On the philosophy of religion, as on all departments of philosophical study, Kant left a deep impress ; and since his own religious training was Christian, and he was familiar with no religion other than the Christian ; since moreover it was of the doctrines of Christianity that he offered a philosophical interpretation in his principal book upon religion, his philosophy was certainly a philosophy of the Christian religion, and its consideration relevant to the studies which the present writer is appointed to direct.

Kant himself has enumerated [1] the topics of philosophical inquiry as three : What can I know ? What ought I to do ?   What may I hope ?

The first question, he says, is purely speculative, the second purely practical, the third at once practical and theoretical. In his view Religion is concerned with the answer to the third question, in which the interest of the speculative or theoretical reason, the

---

[1] *Kr. der r. V.* (H. iii. 532).

interest, that is to say, of Science, and the interest of the practical reason, of Morality, are combined. It was a feature of our experience which especially struck Kant that between the world revealed by dispassionate scientific investigation and the world required by the demands of the moral consciousness there seems to be a discordance, even an incompatibility ; and herein lies, according to him, the impulse to seek a reconciliation of the two in the religious faith that the world of fact is in the last resort subject to the government of those laws which reveal themselves to us as imperative principles of action, and to which we cannot fail to conform ourselves without incurring self-reproach.

To appreciate the position of Kant in the history of the philosophy of religion it is well to bear in mind his threefold division of the interests of human reason into the scientific, the moral, and the religious; and to remember that the especial business of philosophy is the quest of an ultimate unity, in default of which—or, at least, in default of a conviction that an ultimate unity there is, and that it is such as if found would prove to satisfy our reason—our minds are ever restless and discontented, unable to acquiesce either in the apprehension of a world which exists but is indifferent to our moral judgements and aspirations, or in that of a law of duty seeming to prescribe courses of action which, under the conditions of the real world, cannot hope to succeed in achieving their objects. To Kant it seemed clear that, while we could not forgo the quest of such a unity, it was essentially unattainable by the method of Science, and was only apprehensible by faith, or, in other words, belonged to the sphere of Religion.

If we cast back our thoughts to the Middle Ages— and, to understand Kant's historical position aright, it is necessary to do so—we must note in the first place that European thought concerning the real nature of things and the ultimate issues of life was formed under a twofold inspiration, that of Greek Philosophy and that of the Christian Religion. In the second place, we must observe that, before the rediscovery by the scholars of western Europe, in the twelfth and thirteenth centuries of our era, of the greater Aristotelian writings, the general view of the world which had formed the background or framework of their thinking was, on the whole, not that of Greek Philosophy but that traditionally associated with the Christian Religion ; a view which included a transcendent God, the creation out of nothing of a universe whereof the earth was the centre, a drama of redemption culminating in the incarnation of God in Jesus Christ and closing with the last judgement and an endless life of weal or woe in heaven or hell for every individual human soul. Of the two great philosophies of antiquity which, according to the ironical remark of Bacon,[1] survived the deluge of the barbarian invasions because, being less weighty than the rest, they floated on the surface of the waters—the philosophies of Plato and of Aristotle—the latter was at the time

[1] *Nov. Org.* i. 77.

of which I am speaking unknown except for some of the logical treatises which, while affording intellectual stimulus to the keener minds of the age, contained nothing directly inconsistent with the scheme of things suggested by religious tradition ; while the former, the philosophy of Plato, was, if in one way better, yet in another way still less well known than that of his pupil and critic.

The influence of Platonism indeed on the formation of the Christian dogmatic system had been very great ; and thus it indirectly affected the whole tradition which the young nations of Europe had received from their ecclesiastical teachers. Moreover the thought of the theological writer whose individual authority was greater in the western Church than that of any other among the Fathers, St. Augustine, rested on a Platonic foundation, and betrayed throughout the powerful influence exerted upon him in the formative period of his intellectual development by the philosophy of the Neo-Platonic school (as we are now accustomed to call it), of which Plotinus, some of whose writings had made a profound impression upon him, was the greatest master. Not only so, but the *Timaeus* of Plato, in the Latin translation of Chalcidius, was one of the few works of Greek antiquity to which the earlier thinkers of the Middle Ages had access ; and here they might seem to have presented to them something in the nature of a world-view other than that suggested by the Bible. Nor can it be denied that one finds in several authors of the period antecedent to the recovery of the greater Aristotelian works—such as (to name two at random) Bernard Silvestris and Alan of Lille—elements, derived from this source, and from lesser works of the later Roman period which were themselves dependent upon it, not wholly congruous with the Christian tradition. I may mention here in particular the attempts to identify the World Soul of the *Timaeus* with the Holy Spirit of Christian theology, an attempt which, as handled by Abelard, incurred ecclesiastical censure in the early twelfth century. But the figurative and pictorial style of Plato's exposition, combined with the existence of a long-standing tradition which saw in his obscure phrases about the origin of the world a dim adumbration of the facts (as they were assumed to be) recorded in the Book of Genesis, prevented it from having the same effect as the Aristotelian treatises on natural science and metaphysics had at a later date, of exhibiting an articulate view of the world, supported by definite arguments and by an extensive induction from experience, which was obviously at first sight inconsistent in certain important respects with the statements of Scripture and the teaching of the Church.

Again, if there was little or nothing in the Platonic philosophy, so far as known in the earlier Middle Ages, to force upon the attention of those who studied it any incongruity of principle between its view of the world and that commended to them by what they regarded as divine authority, so too there was nothing in it to accentuate that discrepancy

be possible, as some of the Schoolmen thought, so to interpret the expressions of the Philosopher that they should not directly contradict the teaching of the Scripture and the Church on these subjects, it was clear that, along the lines laid down and followed by Aristotle, it would not be possible with the best will in the world to arrive at the dogmas with which they seemed to conflict, or at the central doctrines of Christianity respecting the Trinity in the Godhead and the Incarnation of the Son. Hence it became possible to assign to philosophy a sphere of its own, in which to admit failure to prove all the doctrines of the Church was no disparagement of its powers, since these were necessarily beyond the ken of unassisted natural reason ; and to legitimate the philosopher's independent inquiry into natural fact and into the presuppositions of our natural experience, apart altogether from any such direct ministration to theology as might be afforded by seeing in natural truths or facts types and adumbrations of theological mysteries. Such a mystical interpretation of the world was for the theologian ; it was no part of the business of the philosopher as such.

As our knowledge of the universe was divided into that attainable by natural reason and that for which revelation was needed, so too, in morality, the so-called theological virtues of faith, hope, and charity appeared as a revealed supplement, rendered possible by supernatural assistance, to the cardinal virtues of fortitude, temperance, justice, and prudence, and the other excellences of conduct which the ancient philosophers had, without the aid of revelation, discovered to be necessary to the attainment by man of his natural end.

It is not my present purpose to attempt a criticism of this delimitation of the spheres of Reason and Revelation in religion ;[1] but merely to indicate that it conditions the whole movement of thought which issues in that philosophy of religion which we are about to study. I will now proceed to show in somewhat greater detail how this has been the case.

It must be borne in mind that, according to the Thomist view, natural reason could attain to a knowledge of God, and was thus not a stranger in the sphere of religion. It could conclude, with Aristotle, from the motion of the heaven to an unmoved First Mover thereof, and from the order observed in nature to an ordering Intelligence. It could find out, again with Aristotle, the unity of this Supreme Ruler ; but not the trinity of Persons in this unity, which had been unveiled by the incarnation of the second of these Persons in Jesus Christ ; even although, when this had once been revealed, images and shadows of this truth could be recognized in the trinities discovered elsewhere in nature by the unassisted reason. Thus the modern world did not start with the conception of Science and Religion as two completely dissociated activities of the human spirit ; but with that of a Science which led up to a certain kind of religion, and a supernatural Revela-

[1] I have attempted this in my *Problems in the Relations of God and Man* (1915), pp. 21 foll.

tion which enriched and supplemented this 'natural' religion by the addition thereto of truths which the reason could only receive on authority, though on an authority which had previously accredited itself by proofs satisfactory to reason. It was inevitable that the question should eventually be raised whether the religion in respect of which Reason can rely on its own resources may not be sufficient for salvation ; whether a just God can require of all men a knowledge which is admittedly reserved for a favoured few, and to which no man can apart from special favour attain.

Religion is, it will be observed, regarded, by both parties to the controversy thus aroused, as consisting in, or at least as dependent upon *knowledge*, knowledge of the existence and nature of God. But it would be allowed by both that the perception of the propriety of a certain kind of *behaviour*, congruous with this knowledge, is involved in the possession of this knowledge itself. This behaviour would naturally fall under two heads : the reverence or worship naturally evoked by the knowledge that we are in the presence of so great a Being ; and any conduct which he might be understood to require of us, whether by a supernatural communication of his will or by a natural prompting implanted by him in the hearts of his creatures. This conduct again might be either directed towards God himself (this would concern details of worship), towards ourselves, or towards our fellow men. Those who found a difficulty in justifying the partiality of a supernatural communication not made to all, or in assuring themselves of the actual fact of such a communication, would emphasize the importance of that part of conduct which was suggested by the promptings of our conscience as compared with that supposed to be supernaturally enjoined. This last could be made to wear, in contrast with the other, an air of arbitrariness and irrationality; and where the sanction of the duties alleged to be revealed was represented as consisting in the promise of rewards for their fulfilment and of punishments for their omission, to be awarded in a future life, it was easy to represent the motive to them as selfish in comparison with that which was found in the intrinsic and intuitively perceived excellence of duties which all men could recognize as obligatory; and the virtue exhibited in the performance of which was, it could be urged, its own reward. The famous saying of Spinoza, *Beatitudo non est virtutis praemium, sed ipsa virtus,*[1] had been anticipated a century earlier by the Italian philosopher Pomponazzi in the words [2] *Praemium essentiale virtutis est ipsamet virtus, quae hominem felicem facit.*

But not all those who declined to call in Revelation to the aid of Reason were minded thus to dispense with the motive to virtue provided by the expectation of rewards and punishments in another life. Among the five articles of Natural Religion which are enumerated by Lord Herbert of Cherbury,[3] the reputed

---

[1] *Eth.* v. 42.   [2] *De Immortalitate Animae,* c. 14, p. 120.
[3] *de Veritate* (ed. 1633, pp. 208 foll.).

father of Deism (he was the elder brother of the poet George Herbert), we find this : ' That rewards and punishments are to be expected from God's goodness and justice both in the present and also in a future life.' The whole list is of some importance as an early programme of that kind of ' natural religion ' or, to use Kant's own phrase, ' religion within the limits of mere reason ' which finds its last great exponent in the philosopher of Königsberg himself, whose discussion of the matter is the subject of our present study, ' We must see ', says Lord Herbert, ' what things in Religion are acknowledged by universal consent ; these must all be brought together ; and what things soever all men take for true in religion are then to be reckoned among *notitiae communes.*' They are ultimately stated as follows : 1. That a supreme God exists : 2. That he ought to be worshipped : 3. That the principal point of his worship is moral virtue or the right use of our faculties : 4. That faults or crimes are to be expiated by repentance : 5. That rewards and punishments are to be expected from God's goodness and justice, both in the present and also in a future life.

Not all the representative philosophers of the period which closes in Kant were deists in the sense that they rejected the witness of any historical revelation to the nature of the God of whose existence they held themselves to be assured by natural reason. Descartes, Locke, Leibnitz—to mention three names of the first rank—accepted respectively the teaching of the several Churches in which they were brought up—the Roman Catholic, the Anglican, and the Lutheran—as of divine authority, in all cases sincerely, though not always without reservations on particular points of doctrine. But they all believed, in common with St. Thomas Aquinas and with those who might properly be called deists, that reason, apart from revelation, could assure us by processes of argument, independently of any specifically religious experience, of the existence of a God ; and none of them would have held that a view of the world which left God out would have satisfied the demands of our scientific intelligence. In Professor Wildon Carr's recent book *A Theory of Monads* and in other writings by its learned author will be found emphasized with abundance of illustrations from the philosophical literature of the time the fact that the thinkers of the seventeenth century were accustomed to discuss such problems as those of mind and matter, substance and individuality,—problems which were suggested to them rather by the scientific investigation of natural phenomena than by an experience specifically religious,—in relation to the conception of a transcendent God, which they assumed to be familiar to their readers and unquestionably relevant to their inquiries.[1]

Herein they obviously differed from their suc-

[1] Cp. my paper in a Symposium on the 'Idea of a Transcendent Deity ' in *Concepts of Continuity*, 1924, Arist. Soc. Supplementary vol. iv.

cessors in our own day. Everybody knows the story of the astronomer Laplace's reply to Napoleon when the emperor observed that he had made no mention of God in his *Mécanique céleste* : ' Sire, I had no need of that hypothesis.' Every scientific writer now, however convinced he might personally be of the existence of God, would agree with Laplace in considering a reference to him as out of place in a scientific explanation of natural phenomena. And although in philosophy, which does not, like science (as we now use the word), abstract from all features of experience but those susceptible of treatment under certain categories, the mention of God is felt to be less out of place, yet nowadays one expects to find that supreme unity which it is the business of philosophy to seek, wherein ' we live and move and have our being ', spoken of by such titles as ' the Absolute ', ' Reality ', or the like, rather than by the name of ' God ', except where it is definitely intended to invite us to recognize the presentation to the human soul of this object of metaphysical inquiry as legitimately eliciting therefrom the response of religious awe and reverence.

It is no doubt historically true that it is in Religion that man first concerns himself at all with this background of all his experience ; and Philosophy is therefore, as has justly been said, the daughter of Religion, and starts upon her career with an outfit of questions suggested by religious experience. This, which is true of philosophy in general, is true also of the philosophy of modern Europe. She was at first inclined to take for granted the notion of God with which Christianity had made her familiar, and only gradually did she come to recognize that this notion included more than could be verified by non-religious experience.

The relation of Morality to Religion is a subject which I have discussed at length elsewhere.[1] They have often widely diverged from one another ; but they are, though not to be identified, intimately connected in their origin ; they have never been indifferent to one another ; and in their most highly developed forms are manifestly incomplete each without the other. During the period preceding Kant, the *seculum rationalisticum*, as Mark Pattison called it,[2] when the dominant interest in mathematical and physical science had made men apt to neglect whatever was deficient in the ' clearness and distinctness ' characteristic of mathematical ideas, there was a tendency to exalt Morality at the expense of Religion, on the ground that moral convictions possessed a greater simplicity and intelligibility and challenged more successfully a general assent than religious doctrines, about which men, agreed on the whole in their views of what was (apart from religion) right or wrong, were often found hopelessly at variance, and which moreover were often (as in the case of the dogmas of the Trinity, of the Atonement,

[1] *Problems in the Relations of God and Man* (1915), pp. 104 foll. : *A Century of Anglican Theology and other Lectures*, pp. 55 foll.

[2] ' Tendencies of Religious Thought in England, 1688–1750 ' (*Essays and Reviews*, p. 259).

or of the Real Presence in the Eucharist) distinguished by their inconsistency with the usual assumptions of common sense. But the same temper as led to this exaltation of Morality at the expense of Religion induced also a tendency to justify Morality itself as promoting individual happiness, even if only in the refined form of a quasi-aesthetic satisfaction in the contemplation of a noble action, one's own or another's.

At the same time, just as the idea of God in the minds of the thinkers of this age was inevitably at bottom that to which the Christian Church had accustomed the nations which it had educated, even though certain features of that idea might be consciously abandoned ; so too the Morality which appealed to them was at bottom the Morality taught by the Christian Church, though again with certain modifications, especially in those departments in which the great movement of which the Renaissance and the Reformation were alike aspects had revolted from certain medieval traditions.

In studying Kant's philosophy of religion we must bear in mind these characteristics of the preceding period. In a complete treatment of the subject it might be proper to dwell at length upon his celebrated criticism of the teleological, cosmological, and ontological arguments for the existence of God. This I do not propose to do, partly because I have discussed this already elsewhere ; [1] but also because what Kant aimed at establishing by that criticism

[1] *Problems in the Relations of God and Man* (1915), pp. 159 foll.

is precisely that those arguments do not succeed in proving what they were alleged to prove by those who put them forward, and that upon that account God must be conceived as the object not of knowledge but of faith, that is to say, of a conviction which has practical but not theoretical value, obliging to a course of action, but not adding to our scientific information. It is the distinctive feature of his philosophy of religion that it teaches us to seek in our moral consciousness and there alone the essence of Religion ; for although in Religion there is, according to him, as I have already pointed out, a certain connexion established between practice and theory, which are otherwise at odds, it is a connexion in which the practice determines the theory and not the theory the practice.

In the chapters which follow I shall first give some account of Kant's personal attitude towards the problems of Science, Morality, and Religion. I shall then touch very briefly on his criticism of the dogmatic rational theology which he found in possession of the schools, and attempt to show what he was at various times prepared to offer as a substitute for their proofs of the existence of a Being to whom the sentiment of religious reverence could be rightly directed. I shall dwell more at length on the manner in which he held that moral experience suggested and required a statement in religious language. I shall describe and comment on the detailed account of such a statement given in his treatise on *Religion within the Limits of mere Reason.*

D

I shall say something of the further development of his views on this subject contained in the so-called *Opus postumum*, of which Professor Adickes has lately supplied us with an account ; and I shall end with some observations upon the most salient features of Kant's philosophy of religion and upon its significance and value for us to-day.

II

KANT AND RELIGION

KANT was, by his own account, which there is no real ground for questioning—although patriotic Prussians have done so in their unwillingness to allow any share in him to another nation—on his father's side of Scottish descent.[1] He was of humble parentage, his father being a poor saddler. His superior education he owed to the assistance of Schultz, an eminent Pietistic clergyman of his native town, the university city of Königsberg, the university of which at that time, the university of Berlin not having been founded, was the only one in Prussia proper, though that of Halle, founded by the first King of Prussia, and the fountain-head of the Pietistic movement to which, as we shall see, Kant owed so much, lay also within the dominions of the Hohenzollern dynasty. Kant's parents seem to have been members of Schultz's congregation ; their religion was no doubt affected through him by the Pietism of which he was a prominent representative ; and the school, *Collegium Fridericianum*, of which he was the principal, and in which Kant was educated under his auspices, was known as a centre of Pietistic influence. This fact is not without significance for the understanding of Kant's attitude towards the problems of the philosophy of religion.

[1] See a careful review of the evidence by Dr. Walter Ehmer in an article on ' Kants Abstammung ', published in *Kant-Studien*, xxx, pp. 464 foll. (1925).

Pietism stood for moral earnestness and strict discipline ; it laid stress on a life of devotion and prayer ; and it encouraged in its disciples the ex-pectation of a conscious conversion as the climax of a struggle against sin. We shall observe the effects of Pietism in Kant's conception of religion alike in the way of direct influence and also in that of revolt against its influence. His profound sense of the urgency of the moral law written in our hearts ; the individualism characteristic of his ethical outlook ; his conviction that not gradual improvement but a complete change of orientation is involved in the passage from a bad to a good life ; his appreciation of the ' radical evil ' in human nature, the corruption of the heart, which is none the less certain that it defies satisfactory explanation ; not to mention his obvious familiarity with the Bible ; in all these features of his mind and character we trace the result of his religious education in Pietistic surroundings. On the other hand, in his marked disposition to suspect those who indulge themselves in a supposed personal intercourse with God in prayer of a harmful and demoralizing self-illusion we may not unreasonably conjecture that we see the effects of a reaction from the atmosphere of overstrained absorption in private spiritual ex-perience which the type of religion associated with the Pietistic movement would naturally tend to create. After his matriculation in the university, at the age of sixteen, in 1740, the influence of one Martin Knutzen would seem to have determined him to devote his attention almost wholly to mathematical and physical studies ; and to the assiduous cultivation of the natural bent of his mind in this direction we can trace the development of that tendency to find the sole ideal of knowledge in the kind of knowledge which is attained in mathematical and physical science ; a tendency which, when confronted with his inexpugnable sense of the supreme claim of the moral law upon our obedience, made him so impressive an exponent of the discord between the deterministic world unveiled by science and the world of spiritual freedom into which we are summoned by our conscience ; a discord the resolution of which he sought, as we shall see, in Religion. In Religion,—but, according to the distinction so much in vogue in the eighteenth century, in Natural, not in Revealed Religion. There were two characteristics of Kant's mind which made it natural for him to divert his attention from Revealed Religion as such. One was that revulsion in him, of which I have already spoken, against anything in religious practice which savoured of what he called *Schwärmerei*—fanaticism, that is, or ' enthusiasm ', in the dyslogistic sense in which the word was commonly used at that period to express the abandonment of common sense under the influence of a spiritual intoxication unfavourable no less to moral rectitude than to accurate thought. The other was the markedly *unhistorical* temper of his mind, to which I shall often have to call attention, and in which, as in some other respects, he presents a striking resemblance to the contemporary French Revolution, whose analogue in the realm of thought his philosophy may be said to have been. For the antithesis between the historical and the general or abstract element in religion is perhaps that which for us may be said to have taken the place of the antithesis of Revealed and Natural Religion as it was insisted upon at the period of its greatest vogue.[1]

It is a remarkable proof of the force of Kant's genius that in respect both of the theory of Art and of that of Religion he was able to make the impression that he did, notwithstanding an undeniable deficiency, due in part to his temperament and in part to his circumstances, of what may be called opportunities of aesthetic and religious experience respectively. With Science and with Morality one feels that Kant was completely at home ; no one has better than he comprehended the ideal of the investigator of abstract relations, no one has more whole-heartedly confessed the power of her inexorable demands whom Wordsworth, in Kant's spirit and probably under the indirect influence of his teaching, has called the ' stern daughter of the voice of God '. With Aesthetics, and with Religion as distinct from Morality the case is otherwise. The circumstances of his life denied to Kant any extensive experience of visible beauty, whether natural or wrought by art. He never went beyond the boundaries of East Prussia. He never saw mountains or the ocean ;

[1] Cp. *Problems in the Relations of God and Man* (1915), pp. 58 foll.

nor any of the great achievements of architecture,
painting, or sculpture. He had no great taste for
music ; he is said to have preferred the military kind
to any other and seldom—in later life never—
attended concerts or other public performances.
Nor does anything we know of him suggest that
he was himself an artist, whose native imagination
could dispense with these external stimulants. Yet
the first part of the *Kritik der Urtheilskraft*, in which
he considers the nature of our judgements of taste,
is a work of the highest importance in the history
of aesthetic theory. As to Religion, it is certain
that after early youth he avoided religious exercises.
Only at the call of official duty, when filling the
office of Rector of his University, could he be
induced to attend public worship, the utility of which
he however defends on grounds which we shall
afterwards consider. He thought that any man would
be ashamed to be found upon his knees alone ; he
even remarks, in a note on Prayer communicated to
a certain Professor Kiesewetter who came to Königsberg to sit at his feet in the years 1778-9 and 1791,[1]
that with a real advance in goodness there goes a
disuse of prayer—an observation which it would be
hard to justify from a considerable survey of
Christian experience. While his sentiment of
reverence in the presence alike of ' the starry
heavens above, and the moral law within ', to quote
his famous saying, was profoundly religious, and
while he applies the injunction to ' pray without

[1] H. iv. 505.

ceasing ' to the encouragement of an all-pervading ' spirit of prayer ' in the performance of the duties of our vocation,[1] he deeply distrusted the articulate and ceremonial expression of this spirit on particular occasions as always fraught with danger to the purity of our moral motives and to the honesty and reasonableness of our outlook on the world. Yet, with all this (as one may say) congenital incapacity for much that is most characteristically religious, his great book on *Religion within the Limits of mere Reason* is epoch-making in theology.

But before turning to the consideration of this work it will be necessary to touch upon his criticism of the dogmatic rational theology which he found in possession of the schools ; although, as I said, I do not propose to enter upon a detailed account of his discussion of the so-called proofs of the existence of God, with which I have dealt elsewhere, and which indeed has only an indirect bearing upon his philosophy of religion, properly so called.

[1] H. vi. 294.

III

KANT'S PHILOSOPHY OF RELIGION : THE PRE-CRITICAL PERIOD

THE earliest published reflections of Kant on the philosophy of religion are chiefly concerned with the impression of design made upon us by the spectacle of nature. This seems to have been always in his eyes the most obvious and natural means by which the thought that there is a God is suggested to the human mind. Despite the severe criticism which he brought to bear upon all the formal arguments which had been devised to exhibit this impression as compelling us to adopt the conclusion that God exists as scientifically or philosophically established ; despite his insistence that it was the experience of moral obligation and not the study of natural phenomena which alone could raise the existence of God from the position of a problem, set to us indeed by the natural movement of our intelligence, but beyond the power of our understanding satisfactorily to solve, to that of the object of a reasonable faith, upon which we are not only justified in acting, but are bound to act ; despite all this, Kant constantly affirmed the strength of the *impression* of design made upon us by the spectacle of nature as something which, as it was antecedent to any scholastic *argument* suggested thereby, so it

E

does not cease to exist with the detection of a fallacy in all such arguments.

Even in the treatise on *The General Natural History and Theory of the Heavens*,[1] published in 1755, when he was only thirty-one, he had laid down the lines which are familiar to those who have followed his later discussions ; at once strongly emphasizing the inevitable recognition of the hand of God in the order and harmony of the universe as revealed to the student of the Newtonian system ; and at the same time contending for the possibility of accounting for its actual arrangement, perfect and beautiful as it is, according to the general laws of the system itself, by the opposite forces of centripetal contraction and centrifugal repulsion, without the intervention of a ' *strange* hand '.[2]   The consideration, now so familiar, that such a conception of the universe is worthier of the divine wisdom than one which should require the constant intervention by what, in contrast to the necessary effects of abiding principles of motion, must be called miracles, is here urged with an eloquence which in the works of Kant's later years is very rarely allowed to illuminate his pages. In his defence of this position he probably had in view a notion of Newton's, upon which Leibnitz had already severely animadverted, that, under the general laws of nature, the reciprocal action of comets and planets on one another introduced into the system of nature very small irregularities which would probably in process of time increase more

[1] H. i. 207 foll.   [2] H. i. 314.

and more until the present system shall need the hand of a repairer. As Leibnitz remarked,[1] according to this view ' the machine of God's making is so imperfect that he is obliged to clean it now and then by an extraordinary concourse and even to mend it as a clockmaker mends his work ; who must consequently be so much the more unskilful a workman as he is oftener obliged to mend his work and set it right '.

It would appear however that Kant's obvious earnestness in the contention that a self-regulating universe suggests a higher idea of the divine wisdom than one in need of occasional repair by its Creator did not wholly avert the suspicion that a God whose action could not be distinguished from that of the general laws of nature would not long be regarded as the object of religious reverence. To this suspicion some colour would be lent by the existence of an irreligious deism, described by the then highly influential philosopher Christian Wolf [2] as denying that God cared for the affairs of men or imposed duties upon them. For it is probable that the arguments of the *Allgemeine Naturgeschichte*, perhaps in combination with the fact that the author's preoccupation with physical and mathematical science had by now diverted him altogether from the theological studies in which in his earliest student days he had engaged, were the grounds which induced his old master Schultz, when consulted in

---

[1] *Correspondence of Leibnitz and Clarke* (1717), p. 5.
[2] *Theol. Nat.*, P. ii, § 2, cap. 2, § 564 (ed. 1737; p. 547).

1756, the year after its publication, as to his fitness
for a professorial appointment, to send for him and
ask him ' Whether he feared God from his heart ? '
and only on receiving a satisfactory reply to this
question to consent to act as his sponsor in the
matter.

It is not unworthy of notice that in a treatise, to
the consideration of which I shall afterwards turn,
written eight years after the *General Natural History*, Kant himself shows some hesitation about the
view there put forward of a self-working system as
essentially *better* than one interrupted by miracles ;
and observes that it is the attainment of the end,
not its attainment by certain means, that makes a
system *good*. In human affairs, he points out, there
is, owing to the greater trouble given by doing oneself what one can get done for oneself by machinery,
an advantage belonging to the latter alternative
which has no parallel in the case of a divine agent.[1]

But whatever his views on this matter, there is no
doubt that Kant could, not only in 1756 but ever
afterwards, have given in all sincerity an affirmative
reply to the question which Schultz then put to him.
With all his increasingly clear insight into the
imperfections of the argumentation by which Wolf
and other philosophers of that school (in which he
was still at this date, according to his own confession, enjoying a ' dogmatic slumber ') proved to
their own satisfaction the existence of a God im-

---

[1] *Der einzig mögliche Beweisgrund zu einer Demonstration des
Daseins Gottes*, H. ii. 151, 2.

posing duties upon men and entitled to their worship, neither at that time nor in his later or so-called ' critical ' period did he cease to experience the impression of design, that is of a divine wisdom manifested in nature—an impression which Darwin a century afterwards described himself as feeling strong upon him from time to time though sometimes it seemed to fade away altogether.[1] Nor did he dissociate the witness borne to God by the ' starry heavens ' from that borne by the moral law, or doubt that the wisdom before the revelation of which in the former he stood, in his own phrase, astounded, was one with the holiness unveiled in the ideal set before us by the ' categorical imperative ' of duty speaking through the voice of conscience. In fact it was, I think it may truly be said—although I am not here pretending to use his own language— precisely in the identity of the sentiment of religious awe and reverence evoked in our spirits by the spectacle of nature with that aroused by the consciousness of a law which it is our duty to obey and in our response whereto alone we can find our own true dignity as free personalities that Kant found himself in view of a principle wherein was the promise of a reconciliation between the discordant ideals of the speculative and the practical reason, capable of satisfying that quest for an ultimate unity which our reason can never bring itself to abandon, but which the facts of experience seem continually to disappoint.

[1] *Life and Letters*, i, p. 316 n.

It was eight years after the publication of the *Allgemeine Naturgeschichte* that Kant, still unconverted from ' dogmatism ' to ' criticism ', put forth a treatise with the title *Der einzig mögliche Beweisgrund zu einer Demonstration des Daseins Gottes*, ' The Only Possible Ground of Proof for a Demonstration of the Existence of God '. It may perhaps surprise those unacquainted with the course taken by Kant's thought on this subject prior to the appearance of the *Critique of Pure Reason* to find that this ' only possible proof ' is a modified form of what is called the Ontological Argument.

We must here recall the criticism which in the *Critique of Pure Reason* was hereafter to be levelled against three well-known arguments for the existence of God. The first of these is the Physico-Theological Proof, that is to say, the argument from design. The second is the Cosmological Proof, which argues from the existence of things which are contingent, that is, which we can conceive not to exist and so are impelled to ask *why* they exist, to the existence of a *necessary* Being, on which they depend, and which itself cannot be conceived not to exist. The third and last is the Ontological Proof, which infers from the fact that we can form the notion of a most perfect Being the existence of this Being, since, existence being itself a perfection, without which such a Being would be less perfect, the notion of a most perfect Being that did not exist would be self-contradictory.

While Kant holds (in the *Critique of Pure Reason*)

that this last-mentioned argument is of all the three
the most obviously fallacious, he nevertheless contends that apart from it the other two can be shown
to fail in the attempt to prove what they profess to
prove, namely the existence of such a Being as we
understand by the word God. For the Argument
from Design can only at the best prove some (not
necessarily only one) wise (not necessarily all-wise)
shaper of the universe (not necessarily a creator of
the matter which he shaped); and therefore only
seems to prove the existence of such a Being as we
mean when we talk of God, if we read into this
Architect of the Universe the Necessary or Self-
existent Being of the Cosmological Argument. And
again, he goes on to argue, this Necessary or Self-
existent Being need not be taken to be other than
the World itself as a whole, unless we identify it
with the Supremely Perfect Being of the Ontological
Argument. Hence the fallacy which he finds in
that argument, the fallacy of supposing that existence is a ' perfection ' or predicate beside other
predicates, is really fatal to the other arguments too,
since these cannot prove without the help of the
Ontological Argument what they profess to prove.
This fallacy is involved in the supposition, implied
in that argument, that anything is changed in the
thought or conception of a thing by the fact of its
existence. There is no more in the *conception* of
a hundred dollars which are in my pocket than in
that of a hundred dollars of which a beggar might
dream. Their real existence, though making all the

practical difference in the world, is not one of the predicates which go to make up that conception, such as for example their yellowness. Or, to put it another way, if I conceive them at all, I conceive them as being real ; whether they *are* real or not, does not affect the *conception* ; it is a difference in the relation of the conception to fact. I do not here propose to point out the objections which may be raised against Kant's treatment of the Ontological Argument ; I have, as I said before, dealt with them elsewhere ; I am only concerned to indicate what that treatment was.

In the earlier treatise with which we are now concerned, we find that Kant had already arrived at the conclusion that the form of the Ontological Argument which he found in use was invalid, because of the treatment of ' existence ' as a particular predicate alongside of others. But he thought that a no less *a priori* demonstration of God's existence could be advanced which would avoid this defect. Briefly stated, this ' sole argument ' is that something is *possible*, that any possibility presupposes a real being, and that in this way the existence of a real being antecedent to any mere possibility of the existence of anything else is demonstrable from the very fact of possibility.

The ultimate inseparability of thought from reality, the recognition that a thought which is not a thought of reality is no thought, is the implication of the Ontological Argument in all its forms. In all it may subserve the interests of Religion by countering those ways of thinking, which, under such names as Positivism, Relativism, and the like, often inhibit, so to say, the minds of those who engage in them from that acknowledgement of an Absolute Reality which religion involves. But in none of its forms is the Argument, without supplementation from the sphere of religious experience, a proof of the existence of God as known in religion ; or, to put the same thing in another way, it cannot by itself prove to one who has or owns to having no religious experience the existence of the object of that experience. And I think it may be said that Kant's modification of it in the treatise now under consideration, even if it be thought to avoid certain unsatisfactory features of the older form of the argument, will not be found any more successful than they in this respect.[1] The tone of the book suggests that Kant was already dissatisfied with what he afterwards rejected as ' rational theology ', but was trying to make the best that he could of it. He expresses here, as in the *Critique of Pure Reason*, his personal respect for the argument from design, despite its logical defects ; and he anticipates a later view of his, which we shall have to consider hereafter, by pointing out the greater difficulty of explaining *organic* than of explaining *inorganic* nature by the action of general laws without the reference of details to the wisdom of a divine Creator. The concluding words of the treatise are extremely

---

[1] An account of it will be found in Wallace's *Kant* in Blackwood's *Philosophical Classics*.

characteristic of Kant's life-long attitude towards the questions discussed therein : ' It is very necessary that one should be convinced of God's existence ; but not so necessary that one should prove it.'

A year later Kant published an essay on a question propounded by the Berlin Academy for a prize competition ; ' the Clearness of the Principles of Natural Theology and Ethics '.[1] This essay anticipates the later distinction of Speculative and Practical Reason in its insistence that knowledge of the True and feelings for the Good must not (as, he remarks, people have now begun to perceive) be confounded with one another. But Morality, it will be noticed, is not yet attributed to the Practical Reason ; in sharp contrast with Kant's later views, it is, as we have seen, placed under the head of *feeling* ; and the future apostle of the Categorical Imperative still regards himself as at one with Hutcheson, the Scottish champion of the ' moral sense ', whom he mentions by name as a pioneer in the right treatment of ethical questions.[2]

In 1766 appeared what is perhaps the most entertaining of Kant's writings, the singular work entitled *Träume eines Geistersehers, erläutert durch Träume der Metaphysik,* 'Dreams of a Ghost-seer, illustrated by Dreams of Metaphysic'.[3] The ghost-seer in question was Swedenborg, in the then current stories of whose feats of clairvoyance Kant had plainly

---

[1] *Untersuchung über die Deutlichkeit der Grundsätze der natürlichen Theologie und der Moral,* H. ii. 281 foll.

[2] H. ii. 308.   [3] H. ii. 323 foll.

taken great interest. I shall content myself with translating the last paragraph of this treatise, which contains the serious lessons that Kant would have us learn from his half-serious, half-ironical discussion of attempts, whether by way of converse with unembodied spirits or by speculation on the possible nature of such beings, to transcend the world of ordinary experience. He confessed in a letter to the Jewish philosopher, Moses Mendelssohn,[1] some attraction to stories of the kind that were related of Swedenborg, as well as a certain disposition to indulge the fancy that the arguments alleged in support of them might turn out to be correct, in spite of the absurdities which discredited the stories and the fantastic and unintelligible notions which discredited the attempts to account for them rationally. He had therefore been directing his satire to some extent against himself. But his conclusion is as follows : [2]

'While on the one hand, when we inquire more deeply, we come to see that it is impossible in these cases to attain to the philosophical insight which could give conviction respecting these things, a calm and unprejudiced mind must also on the one hand admit that such insight can be dispensed with as unnecessary. In our conceit of knowledge we readily excuse our preoccupation with these things by a pretence of their importance ; and so it is commonly pretended that a rational insight into the spiritual nature of the soul is necessary for our conviction of its existence after death and this conviction again as a motive to a virtuous life ; and we add in

[1] H. viii. 672 foll.   [2] H. ii. 380 f.

defence of our idle curiosity that the truth of apparitions of disembodied souls would supply a proof from experience of all these things. But true wisdom goes hand in hand with simplicity and, where the heart guides the understanding in her ways, the pompous apparatus of learning can commonly be dispensed with, and her ends attained without the use of means that can never be at the disposal of all men. How ? Is it only good to be virtuous because there is another world ? Or will not actions rather be rewarded in another world because they were in themselves good and virtuous ? Are there not in the heart of man moral precepts of which we are immediately aware, and must we, in order to set him going in this world in accordance with those precepts, erect our machinery in another world ? Can the man be reckoned just and virtuous who joyfully indulges himself in his favourite vices, if only he be not threatened with future punishment ? Shall we not rather say of such a one that he merely shuns the practice of wickedness while cherishing the vicious disposition in his soul ? that he loves the profit to be had from apparently virtuous conduct but hates virtue itself ? In fact experience teaches us that many who have been taught to believe in a future life and are convinced of its reality nevertheless indulge in vice and baseness, and only trouble themselves about the means of cleverly escaping the future consequences thereof; but there has never lived a well-disposed soul which could bear the thought that there is an end of all at death, and which has not been by noble sentiments exalted to the hope of a future life. It would seem then to agree better with human nature and with purity of morals to base our expectation of the life to come on the sentiments of a well-disposed soul than to reverse this order and base good conduct on our hope of the next world. In this way no room is left for moral faith, which in its simplicity can raise us above many subtleties of reasoning, and which alone is suitable to man in whatever condition he may be, as leading him, by no roundabout road but directly, to the true ends of his being. Let us then leave to idle brains all pretentious doctrines which deal with objects of speculation and concern so far removed from our real interests. They are in fact quite indifferent to us, and the momentary appearance of reasoned arguments for or against them may perhaps be decisive for obtaining assent in the debates of the school, but hardly for the future destiny of an honest man. Human reason is not equipped with wings strong enough to part the lofty clouds which hide from our eyes the secrets of the other world, and our curiosity, which so earnestly endeavours to discover these, may be met by the simple but very natural rejoinder that it is best to make up one's mind to wait patiently till we are there. And since our destiny in the world to come may probably be largely determined by the manner in which we have filled the place assigned to us in this, I conclude with the resolution which Voltaire puts into the mouth of his worthy Candide at the end of so many idle controversies : Let us look after our happiness, go into our garden, and labour there.'

In 1770, on his appointment to the chair of Logic and Metaphysics at Königsberg, which he was to hold for the remainder of his life, Kant inaugurated his professorship by a Latin dissertation *de mundi sensibilis et intelligibilis forma et principiis*,[1] which is generally recognized as marking his final passage from the ' dogmatic ' to the ' critical ' stage of his philosophical development. Here he distinguishes sharply between the Senses and the Understanding.

[1] H. ii. 393 foll.

The world in space and time is what we find it to be, not because things as they exist in themselves independently of us are interconnected in this way, but because our minds are so constituted as only to perceive things thus. The mathematical sciences are certain *a priori* because space and time, with which they are concerned, are forms of our sensibility, and metaphysical difficulties which may be raised about them are irrelevant, since they only relate to things as thus perceived. On the other hand, the conceptions of the understanding, by means of which we apprehend the intelligible or noumenal world, impart a genuine knowledge of this world, the validity of which is not to be questioned on account of difficulties in presenting what belongs thereto—such realities, for example, as God or the soul—under temporal or spatial forms ; for these forms are in no way applicable to these realities, which are objects, not of sense, but of the understanding only.

It will be at once perceived by those acquainted with the doctrine of Kant's *Critique of Pure Reason* that he has not yet in this Inaugural Dissertation of his taken one step, which had to be taken before he could be said to be in full possession of that doctrine. He had not yet denied to the human mind all knowledge, properly so called, of things as they are in themselves apart from our perception of them. The real or noumenal existence of things independently of our perception of them Kant indeed never denied ; but he did come to deny to us any true knowledge of their natures, because he came to hold that the conceptions of the understanding themselves, which in the *Dissertation* he had treated as no less intended to apprehend ultimate reality than the senses to apprehend the world in space and time, were really useless to us outside of that world, except as suggesting to us the possibility of a reality which transcends it and, in transcending it, transcends also our powers of knowledge, conditioned through and through as they are by the sensibility with which our reason is, at least in this life, inseparably yoked together.

The intermediate position of the *Dissertation* between the ' dogmatic ' position of earlier writings, in which Kant had still treated the world in space and time as real in itself, and the completely ' critical ' position, in which he explicitly denied to the human mind the capacity of *knowledge* (though not of *faith*) beyond the limits of that world, brings him nearer than at any other point in the development of his philosophy to the position of Plato. The description of Time in the *Dissertation* as *aeternitas phaenomenon*, because representing in the form of a succession an order which in itself was not successive (Space is correspondingly described as *omnipraesentia phaenomenon*), recalls the famous words in which Plato tells us that Time is ' a moving image of eternity '.[1] And Kant himself, though he makes no express reference to Plato in this connexion, refers to Malebranche's ' seeing of all things in God ' as

[1] *Tim.* 37 D.

a kindred conception to his own ; characteristically excusing himself for venturing into such mystical company beyond those bounds of demonstrative certainty, within which it would be more fitting for metaphysical conception to confine itself. Now Malebranche's doctrine was of course of direct Platonic descent through St. Augustine. It is curious by the way to note that when, as we shall see hereafter, Kant in his old age, being drawn, as the so-called *Opus postumum* shows, toward a less purely transcendent conception of God than had been habitual with him in earlier years, felt himself less out of sympathy than of old with the great immanentist Spinoza, whose influence he saw by that time everywhere growing around him, he more than once attributed, in the papers found on his desk after his death, to that philosopher the phrase of ' seeing all things in God ' which he had well known thirty years before to belong to Malebranche.

But it is doubtful whether, even at the time of the *Dissertation*, Kant's thought was quite so near to Plato's as some of his expressions might seem to imply. The earlier *Dreams of a Ghost-seer* suggests that he already felt more dissatisfaction with current metaphysical theories of God and the soul, even when dissociated from the imaginative revelations of prophets like Swedenborg, than he was prepared to express in the definite and formal language appropriate to an inaugural lecture. And in truth one is somewhat surprised to find him claiming for his own doctrine, in the passage to which I have referred, a kinship with that of Malebranche. He seems to have been struck by the notion that the temporal and spatial order of which we are cognizant, although its actual form of succession and mutual externality is due to the peculiar nature of our cognitive faculties, yet must point beyond itself to an ultimate unity, within which our mind and the external world are correlated with one another; and to an infinite and absolute duration within which the succession of temporal changes takes place; and thus reveals to us the omnipresent and eternal reality, without which the whole process of perception would be impossible. The root idea of Malebranche was rather that illumination by the divine mind is the true account of human knowledge; and the expressions of Kant remind one rather of Newton, an author who exercised far more influence upon him than Malebranche, and his view of Absolute Space as the sensorium of the omnipresent Deity. But no doubt the general reflection that philosophy can never rest content without at least a faith in a divine Wisdom and Goodness, to which all the systematic order that we find in the world is ultimately referable, and in which the oppositions and discordances which we also find are ultimately reconciled, was always the ' fountain light of all ' Kant's ' seeing ', no less than of that of thinkers such as Plato in antiquity and, in the century before his own, Malebranche and Spinoza; thinkers whose mood is very different from his own, and, with whom, whether in their recognition of the capacity of our reason for converse with reality as it is in itself, or in their readiness to discover God or the Good immanent in our ordinary experience, he was more frequently and acutely conscious of difference than of agreement.

There are two passages in the *Dissertation* to which, before passing on, I shall call my readers' attention, because they illustrate very well Kant's attitude toward two questions associated with the philosophy of religion ; the question of the nature of the divine mind and the question of the possibility of what is called miracle.

1. Students of the *Critique of Pure Reason* know that the conception of an *intuitive understanding* is one of considerable importance in Kant's mature philosophy. It is a kind of understanding which, as he contends, we do not possess, but which notwithstanding he regards as conceivable. That he does so regard it is the point which ultimately distinguishes his theory of knowledge from that which Herbert Spencer developed out of his theory as transmitted throught the medium of Sir William Hamilton and Dean Mansel. Herbert Spencer denies to man the possibility of a knowledge of the Absolute on the ground that knowledge as such is a relation between subject and object, so that to speak of a knowledge of what is, by definition, not in relation to anything, is to use meaningless language. Things can only be known as they are in relation to the knower ; not as they are in themselves apart from this relation. It is clear that this argument rejects

the claim not only of *human* knowledge but of *any* knowledge whatever to be the apprehension of things as they are in themselves. It says indeed at bottom no more than that we cannot know things without their being known ; which no one need be concerned to dispute. But it implies a view of knowledge which may be disputed. It implies that knowledge necessarily *alters* what is known ; whereas it might seem rather to be the very meaning of the word *knowledge* that a thing is *not* altered by being known. I do not propose to pursue this subject further at present ; but only to point out that Kant's own censure of human knowledge proceeds on quite a different principle from Spencer's. Not *because it is knowledge* is human knowledge, according to Kant, not a knowledge of things in themselves ; but because human knowledge is always conditioned by the senses, apart from which we have no faculty of intuition or direct perception. Our perceptions or intuitions are always sensible ; our understanding, on the other hand, is never intuitive, but deals only with general notions, which are empty of any contact except so far as this is supplied by experience through the senses or the imagination. There is nothing here to suggest that there may not exist an intuitive understanding, though *our* understanding is not such ; and Kant is generally prepared to acquiesce in the usual supposition that God's understanding is intuitive. In his critical period he would not indeed allow to this attribution of an intuitive understanding to God the value of a piece of knowledge about him, beyond that of indicating that he cannot be supposed subject to the limitations which make it impossible for *our* understanding to be intuitive. In the *Dissertation* however an intuitive understanding is positively ascribed to the divine Being.

> ' The intuitive power (*intuitus*) of our mind is always passive ; and is only possible so far as some object can affect our senses ; but the intuitive power of God, which is not the effect of objects, but their cause (*principium, non principiatum*), since it is independent of them, is their archetype, and hence is completely intellectual.' [1]

This is in accordance with all theological tradition ; and it is a question of much philosophical importance whether we can on any grounds entertain the thought that mind in its own nature is not necessarily obliged to wait upon objects, as we generally conceive our minds to be—for even where we have made an object ourselves, it must be there for us to know it as made—but may itself be creative of its own objects. The historical origin of what is called Idealism has always lain in the attempt to extend to the human spirit what is at first conceived as a prerogative of the divine.

2. Kant accepts, as a principle to be borne in mind in our explanation of phenomena, ' that all things take place according to the order of nature ; not because we possess so complete a knowledge of the occurrence of events in the world according to the common laws of nature that we can perceive clearly

[1] § 10 ; H. ii. 204.

the impossibility or extreme improbability of supernatural occurrences, but because, if once we depart
from the order of nature, our understanding becomes
useless, and a presumptuous readiness to appeal to
supernatural explanations is a pillow for a lazy
understanding '.[1] Here, as hereafter always in Kant,
the assumption of the supernatural is excluded on
' critical ' principles, as inconsistent with the limits
of our understanding, not on the ground that we
are in a position dogmatically to deny its possibility.
We shall be reminded of this attitude when we
come to discuss the theory of Grace in his elaborated
philosophy of religion.

[1] § 30 ; H. ii. 424.

IV

KANT'S PHILOSOPHY OF RELIGION :
PERIOD OF THE CRITIQUES

THE first edition of Kant's *Critique of Pure Reason*[1] appeared in 1781. In the section of this work called the *Transcendental Dialectic* he gives an account of the illusory reasonings which owe their origin to an attempt to employ the categories of the understanding beyond the region of possible experience by means of the senses to which they alone are applicable. These illusory reasonings are described by him as concerned with three *Ideas*, that is to say, conceptions inevitably framed by our Reason in its endeavour to unify and complete the experience which, given to us as it is in space and time, must ever be as it were piecemeal and indefinitely capable of receiving additions.

The third of these Ideas is the Idea of God as the Supreme Being in whom all possible perfections are united in a concrete individuality ; this, in view of this attribution to it of a concrete individuality, is distinguished as the *Ideal* of Pure Reason.

I have already said that I do not propose to deal

---

[1] *Werke*, ed. Hartenstein, vol. iii. The text of the second edition is given, and the differences of the first from the second edition are pointed out in foot-notes. The portions of the first which are omitted from the second are given at the end of the volume.

at length in this book with the detail of Kant's treatment in the *Critique of Pure Reason* of the proofs of God's existence alleged by the ' rational theology ' which he there examines.[1] For one thing I have discussed it elsewhere ; moreover its bearing on Kant's philosophy of religion is only indirect. For it is his very purpose, in this the first of his *Critiques*, to show that the only *theoretical* use which can legitimately be made of the idea of God is, as he calls it, *regulative.* It is to provide us with the notion of a systematic unity of all reality, to serve as the standard which we are to set before ourselves in our study of experience ; so that we may never be content to rest satisfied with regarding the objects of our thought as *ultimately* unconnected and mutually discordant ; but may always, by means of the assumption that they are parts of a wisely planned whole, be led ever onwards in the search for further connexions among them. We may even, so far as it promotes this end, introduce into the idea anthropomorphic elements ; we may think of the universe, as has been suggested above, as designed by a Being possessed of wisdom and power such as exist in man, but raised to the highest possible degree.[2] But precisely what the theoretical reason by itself is not entitled to do is to justify us in supposing ourselves to have increased in this way our knowledge of the actual constitution of the real

[1] Professor Kemp Smith's *Commentary* may be consulted for the development of Kant's thought upon this subject.

[2] *Kr. der r. V.* (H. iii. 468).

world ; and so long as God is no more for us than a *regulative idea* in the Kantian sense, he can scarcely be held to be an object of religious worship. Indeed Kant himself hints [1] that to speak of ' Nature ' instead of ' God ' in this connexion will do as well and even perhaps be less misleading, because suggesting less knowledge of what that Being is which lies behind phenomena. But this is only so long as our moral consciousness is not appealed to. With the moral sentiments, he thinks, the thought of God —and, he adds, that of a future life—is so inextricably interwoven that we need never fear that they will be taken away from us by speculative arguments.[2]

I shall therefore pass on to the theology of Kant's writings on moral philosophy, the teaching of which is however anticipated in the section of the *Critique of Pure Reason* entitled ' The Canon of Pure Reason '.[3]

The poet Heine, in an often-quoted passage of his *Deutschland*,[4] represents Kant as, after carrying farther than his contemporary revolutionaries in France the campaign of rebellion in which they were alike engaged, and slain not merely a king but, by his demolition of the arguments for his existence, the God of the old *régime*, being arrested by the spectacle of his old servant Lampe ' standing by, with his umbrella under his arm, a distressed onlooker, with tears and the sweat of his anxiety

---

[1] *Kr. der r. V.* (H. iii. 468).   [2] *Kr. der r. V.* (H. iii. 546).
[3] H. iii. 526 foll.
[4] *Zur Gesch. der Religion u. Philos. in Deutschland*, 3. Buch ; *Werke*, ed. Lachmann, iii. 80 f.

running down his face'. At this sight Kant 'shows that he is not merely a great philosopher but a good man ; and, after reflection, half good-humouredly, half ironically, he says : " Old Lampe must have a God, otherwise the poor fellow won't be happy. Man should be happy in the world—so says the Practical Reason, so far as I am concerned—therefore the Practical Reason may guarantee the existence of God." In consequence, Kant distinguishes between the theoretical Reason and the practical Reason, and with the latter, as with a magic wand, he brings to life again the corpse of the deism which the theoretical Reason had slain. Did Kant (continues Heine) perhaps perform this resurrection, not merely for old Lampe's sake, but also for that of the police ? Or did he really act from conviction ? Did he, by his destruction of all proofs of the being of God, wish to show us clearly how miserable a thing it is to be able to know nothing of God's existence ? If so, he acted just as wisely as a Westphalian friend of mine, who smashed all the lamps in the Grohnder-strasse at Göttingen, and then, standing there in the dark, delivered a long oration on the practical utility of the lamps, which indeed he had only smashed in order to show us how without them we could see nothing.'

Although Heine is not alone in finding it difficult to believe that Kant's position in this matter could have been one of genuine conviction, I do not think we can genuinely doubt that in fact it was so. Not only did Kant himself, so far as all the evidence

goes, always believe in the existence of God as a
real Being, the source of the order and harmony of
the world, notwithstanding his abandonment of all
the speculative proofs offered thereof, not merely as
actually fallacious but as in principle bound to fail ;
but also, for the greater part of his life at any rate
(I will discuss later on the theory that his *Opus
postumum* implies an alteration of his view at the
end of it), he envisaged this God, in whom he never
ceased to believe, after the fashion of the theism
current in his youth. Unlike some of his contemporaries, such as Lessing among those older than
himself and Goethe among those younger, who were
turning to the long-neglected Spinoza—whom even
the tolerant Locke could only mention [1] as one
whose name was 'justly decried'—as their master
in philosophy, he seems to have found the notion of
an immanent God unfamiliar and uncongenial to his
mind. Yet he was by no means unaware either of
the difficulties inherent in the representation of God
as a transcendent personality, or of some considerations which tell in favour rather of an immanent
purposiveness in nature than of a design related to
the processes whereby it is carried out as that in the
head of a human craftsman or artist is to the work
which he executes in accordance therewith.

   As regards the former, the revulsion of the imagination from the representation of a transcendent God
could hardly be more impressively stated than in

----

[1] *Reply to the Bishop of Worcester's Answer to his Second
Letter* (1699), p. 422.

a passage of Kant's discussion of what he calls the Cosmological Argument for God's existence—the argument, that is to say, from the contingency of all particular things in the world to the existence of a necessary or self-existent Being, upon whom their existence ultimately depends.

' Unconditioned necessity,' says Kant,[1] ' which, as the ultimate support of all things, is to our minds an indispensable supposition, is to the human understanding the veritable Abyss. Even eternity, in all the fearful sublimity of Haller's [2] description of it, does not produce upon us nearly so overwhelming an effect of dizziness ; for it does but *measure* the duration of things, it does not support them. We cannot avoid the thought, nor yet can we endure it, that a Being, which we represent to ourselves as the highest of all possible beings, should, as it were, say to himself : I am from eternity to eternity ; beyond me is nothing except that which exists merely through my

[1] *Kr. der r. V.* (H. iii. 417.)

[2] He is thinking, no doubt, of a passage which he had quoted in his *Allgemeine Naturgeschichte* (H. i. 304), in which the poet addresses Eternity in these words :

Wenn denn ein zweites Nichts wird diese Welt begraben ;
Wenn von dem Alles selbst nichts bleibet als die Stelle ;
Wenn mancher Himmel noch, von andern Sternen helle,
Wird seinen Lauf vollendet haben ;
Wirst du so jung als jetzt, von deinem Tod gleich weit,
Gleich ewig künftig sein wie heut.

which we may perhaps thus translate :

When this world shall to nothingness return,
Nor aught thereof abide but empty space ;
When other heavens, wherein new stars shall burn,
And others yet, have run their destined race,
Thou still as young as now, nor nearer death shalt be,
Nor less than on this day the years reserved for thee.

own will ; *but whence then am I* ? Here everything sinks away from under us and the greatest perfection, no less than the smallest, hangs without support in the presence of the speculative Reason, which finds it cost it as little to let the one vanish away as the other.'

Kant of course meets this situation by his conviction that the notion of a Necessary Being is not to be hypostatized or treated as a real object of thought ; it is only a negative principle, compelling us to be content with nothing short of a complete account in our explanation of the interconnexion of phenomena. But the passage I have quoted shows that not only the logical defects of the arguments for God's existence, but the imaginative difficulties which beset the representation of God as a transcendent real Being, endued with the attribute of self-consciousness, were quite familiar to his mind ; and yet he never, notwithstanding these, ceased to regard that representation as one which we are justified in retaining as corresponding to unquestionable facts of *moral* experience which could scarcely be expressed in any other way.

Again, there is no doubt that Kant, by the time that he published the *Critique of Pure Reason*, was acquainted with Hume's *Dialogues concerning Natural Religion*, which he expressly discusses in the *Prolegomena to all future Metaphysic*,[1] a briefer and more popular account of his critical philosophy, published two years after the *Critique* itself. In these *Dialogues* the chief of Kant's arguments

[1] §§ 57 foll. ; H. iv. 98 foll.

against the current proofs of God's existence—
especially those against the Argument from Design—
are anticipated ; and in this most brilliant statement
of the theme which he was himself—with, it must
be admitted, far less lucidity and grace than his
predecessor—expounding in the sections on the
Transcendental Ideal, the great Scottish thinker
had thrown out the pregnant remark that ' the world
plainly resembles more an animal or a vegetable
than it does a watch or a knitting-loom. Its cause
therefore, it is probable, resembles the cause of the
former. The cause of the former is generation or
vegetation. The cause therefore of the world we
may infer to be something similar or analogous to
generation or vegetation.' [1] This observation of
Philo, one of the characters in Hume's *Dialogues*,
into whose mouth are put the most revolutionary
of his suggestions, strikes us nowadays as far less
perverse than Hume, no doubt from a just perception of the intellectual atmosphere of his own
age, represents it as seeming not only to the orthodox
Demea but to the philosophical though less sceptical
Cleanthes. One might perhaps expect that Kant,
who had long recognized the advantage, for the
purposes of natural science, of being able to explain
phenomena by the general laws of their relations,
as discovered by observation and experiment, without
an appeal to a Designer external to them, would have
welcomed the suggestion that not only the mechanical
system of the heavens, but the world of organic

[1] Part VII.

growth, which seemed to him at present to defy any such explanation, might be regarded as self-explanatory, and even as suggesting a better analogy for the origin of the whole universe than that of the contrivance of a mechanism. But it belonged to the cautious and deliberate temper of his mind that he was never disposed to embrace with a ready welcome trains of reflection that could not easily be adjusted to his previous convictions and habits of thought ; and we have to wait for the so-called *Critique of the Faculty of Judgement* (*Kritik der Urtheilskraft*) to see him wrestling with the problem of teleology in relation to the organic world. Hume himself, despite his acute exposure, both in the *Dialogues* and in his *Natural History of Religion*, of the difficulties of the current theology, seems to have remained at bottom a theist on the ground of the general impression of design made by nature upon the mind of an unprejudiced observer. ' Surely, where reasonable men treat these subjects,' says even the sceptical Philo, ' the question can never be concerning the Being, but only the Nature of the Deity. The former truth . . . is unquestionable and self-evident. Nothing exists without a cause ; and the original cause of this universe (whatever it be) we call God, and piously ascribe to him every species of perfection. Whoever scruples this fundamental truth, deserves every punishment which can be inflicted among philosophers, to wit, the greatest ridicule, contempt, and disapprobation.' [1]   And,

[1] *Dialogues*, Pt. II.

despite the fact that Philo's objections to most of the usual theses of the expounders of Natural Theology are never answered, Pamphilus, the auditor of the dialogues, is made to conclude that, ' as nothing ever made a greater impression on me than all the reasonings of that day ; so I confess that, upon a serious review of the whole, I cannot but think that Philo's principles are more probable than Demea's ; but that those of Cleanthes '—a theist, though unorthodox—' approach still nearer to the truth '.[1]   But if even Hume, as these passages suggest,—and there is other evidence to support this view of his real position—never abandoned a belief in God as the ultimate Author of nature, of whom we can know little, but whom we are justified in venerating, Kant was so much the less likely to do so, as the evidence for his existence from the moral experience of mankind appeared to him far more weighty than it did to Hume, on account of his very different conception of the character of that experience itself ; to which we must now turn.

The most striking statement of Kant's ethical doctrine is that contained in the treatise published in 1783 under the title *Grundlegung zur Metaphysik der Sitten* (a phrase translated in Dr. Abbott's *Kant's Theory of Ethics* as *Fundamental Principles of the Metaphysic of Morals*) ;[2] although we do not find developed in this work the theological interpretation of that doctrine which he afterwards propounded in his *Critique of Practical Reason*.   I am assuming in

[1] Ibid., Pt. XII, ad fin.   [2] H. iv. 235 foll.

my readers a general acquaintance with Kant's philosophy and shall therefore do no more than recall the outstanding features of the Kantian ethics. They are decisively distinguished from any hedonism, however qualified or disguised, which should, even in the last resort, ' when we sit down in a cool hour ' (to use an expression of Butler's),[1] find the ultimate sanction of morality in the pleasure—or in the freedom from pain—that it may bring, by the uncompromising assertion that morality is always a *categorical imperative*, that is to say, a command about which there is nothing conditional or hypothetical. It does not bid us ' Do this, if you would be happy ', but *Do this*—not for any ulterior reason, but *because it is your duty*. The ordinary moral consciousness, so Kant powerfully urges, always in fact regards disinterested obedience to such a law as essential to a truly moral action. The man who, but for some anticipated advantage, would not do his duty, is so far forth not acting morally, although he may be doing that which he would do, if he were so acting. To put the question—not why this or that is one's duty, but—why one should do one's duty is the same thing as to repudiate duty altogether, to be immoral. Our moral consciousness, our consciousness of *obligation*, is something absolutely different from any experience of the sequence of certain effects upon certain kinds of action. It is vain to seek for evidence that such and such actions are

---

[1] *Sermon* XI. Butler does not himself endorse this ultimate hedonism. See Prof. A. E. Taylor in *Mind* for July 1926, p. 295.

right or wrong in the experience of what men have done or do. Although no man had ever obeyed the law, that would not in the least affect its claim upon us. The expression *I ought* represents an experience which is ultimate and self-explanatory ; and in any attempt to get, so to speak, behind it, the true nature of it is let slip, and it becomes a mere illusion, in which appetite or self-interest masquerades as something quite different ; an illusion moreover which would still leave it quite unaccounted for how we came at all by an idea so wholly unlike what, if we had it not already, anything *else* could generate.

I am of course well aware of many explanations that have been offered, both before and since the time of Kant, of this unique experience, which would deprive it of the peculiar character which he attributes to it ; but I am not now discussing the Kantian ethics, except by the way ; and I shall content myself for the present with saying that, while there are details in Kant's account of our moral experience which appear to me open to question, I believe that he is in the main matter absolutely in the right ; and that no one else has so clearly ascertained and described the essential nature of that experience, by which it is distinguished from all other experience whatsoever.

Upon this Kantian doctrine I shall however make certain observations, the importance of which for our subject will appear more fully later on. Kant has often been criticized, and not wholly without justice, for the extreme abstraction of the sense of duty from its emotional and social context to which he was led by his desire to secure the notion of the morally *right* from the confusion of it, actually present in so many ethical theories, with the sentimentally agreeable or the politically useful. But his critics have sometimes been inclined to represent the Kantian ethics as mere *theory* in contrast with a concrete realization of the good life in social institutions, thus taking Kant to stand for what Hegel called *Moralität* in distinction from *Sittlichkeit* ; or again as mere *legalism*, as the ethics of the policeman, uninspired by any positive enthusiasm.[1] I cannot but think that neither description does justice to Kant's ethical teaching. It is especially relevant to the subject of Kant's philosophy of religion to note that, whatever we may find wanting in Kant's account of the relation of morality to other aspects of human life, his own attitude towards the moral law is always profoundly *religious*, full of that sentiment of awe and self-prostration which we associate with the perception anywhere of what Professor Otto has lately taught us to call *das Numinose*. And I would further point out a connexion, which I think it not merely fanciful to trace between a characteristic feature of Kant's ethical theory and the Pietistic teaching which he received in youth, and which, widely as he departed from

[1] Cp. an article on ' Bernard Bosanquet's Philosophy of Religion ' contributed by me to the *Hibbert Journal* for Oct. 1923, p. 87.

the dogmatic system associated with it, never ceased to colour his outlook upon life.

This feature is one which at once strikes students of Kant's ethics as differentiating them from those of Aristotle. There was no portion of the latter which Kant more decisively rejected than the famous ' doctrine of the mean '. It may indeed be doubted whether Kant fully appreciated the actual place of that doctrine in Aristotle's own system, or the qualifications with which it was held by him—but, as he found it, it seemed to him to make the difference between badness and goodness merely quantitative,[1] so that one could pass from one to the other by slight degrees, by just doing a certain sort of action ever less and less, or a certain other sort ever more and more, without that need of a radical change of *direction*, if one may so speak, which appeared to him to be implied in the radical difference between the ' good will ', the will to do what is right, what is one's duty, whatever that may be, quite apart from any consideration of my own pleasure or interest, and the will to get by what I do an individual satisfaction, however refined and intellectual my tastes, however generally useful the results of my activities. The moral experience is presented by Kant as always, in the first place, one of the infinite and absolute claim of the moral law upon our obedience. Afterwards one may discover that, when we reflect upon it, this may involve a recognition of

[1] See *Tugendlehre*, Einleitung xiii, and ibid. § 10 ; H. vii. 207, 238 foll.

our equality with all others who are aware of a like claim upon them—and ultimately of our fellowship with them in a spiritual commonwealth, wherein this law is supreme ; but primarily it is an experience individual and even solitary ; and in this respect it undoubtedly corresponds to the experience called *conversion* among Pietists and those of similar religious views.   Thus, remote as Kant's whole bent in his maturity was from any emphasis upon such emotion as usually attends ' conversion ', none the less his ethics were attuned to that experience, and can hardly perhaps be completely understood from within by any one to whom that experience is utterly strange or alien ; although we must not overlook the fact that (as readers of James's *Varieties of Religious Experience* will not need to be reminded) crises which are psychologically indistinguishable from the ' conversions ' familiar in certain Christian communities may occur altogether apart from the convictions by which such new orientations are interpreted by those communities.

Three years after the *Grundlegung* had indicated the fashion in which Kant envisaged our moral experience, he set side by side with the *Critique of Pure Reason* a *Critique of Practical Reason*, in which our knowledge of our duty was investigated on the same lines as those which had been followed in the earlier examination of our knowledge of nature, that is, of the world which confronts us in time and space. Too much stress is not to be laid upon the parallelism which Kant aimed at establishing between the two inquiries ; for his passion for what we may, after Kant himself, call ' architectonic ' often misled him into illusory attempts to discuss various subjects on one detailed plan, issuing occasionally—especially in the later *Kritik der Urtheilskraft*—in vain repetitions rendered necessary merely by the supposed obligation of constructing anything that was to be called a *Critique* on the same plan as that adopted in the first work to which he had given the name. But the general contrast of the Theoretical and the Practical Reason was no mere formality. In the universality and necessity which distinguished the obligation of duty is revealed its essentially rational character ; all properly *human* and therefore not merely instinctive volition is indeed ' practical reason ', as implying a *reason* for what is willed ; but in moral action, so far as it is truly such, the only motive present is the recognition of it as embodying a law which is one and the same for all rational beings. Moreover not only is this manifestation of Reason in the consciousness of Duty no less for Kant a genuine manifestation of Reason than is the apprehension in the sciences of what is necessarily true ; it has, as he puts it, the *primacy* over the speculative or theoretical Reason, in that it has to do with the whole life of all men, whereas the pursuit of abstract truth is only a department of the life of some men.

The general account given of the nature of morality in the *Critique of Practical Reason* does not vary from that previously given in the *Grundlegung* ;

but it is followed up by a discussion of the *Summum Bonum* or Highest Good—already adumbrated in the *Critique of Pure Reason* [1]—in connexion with which Kant's peculiar notion of Religion as an appendix to Ethics comes into view. With this notion we shall have to concern ourselves for the greater part of his account of his philosophy of religion ; and in entering upon its consideration we must remind ourselves that, although Kant assigns to Religion, under that name, as a distinct activity of the human spirit, this secondary or subordinate place, we shall not obtain an adequate or perfectly balanced view of his position in regard to Religion if we ever forget that his attitude toward the Moral Law itself is essentially a profoundly religious attitude, and is quite misunderstood if identified, as too often it is, with any legalism that could be justly contrasted with a religious morality as self-complacent or unspiritual.

Turning to Kant's doctrine of the *Summum Bonum* as expounded in the *Critique of Practical Reason*, [2] we find him distinguishing two senses in which we may speak of a *Summum Bonum*, *Höchste Gut*, or Supreme Good. We may mean by this expression either *das Oberste Gut* or *Supremum Bonum* ; or, on the other hand, *das Vollendete Gut* or *Bonum Consummatum*. By the former he means *bonum originarium*, a good which is good in its own right, not only as a means to, or requisite condition of, some

[1] *K. der r. V.* (H. iii. 531 foll.).
[2] *Kr. der pr. V.* (H. v. 116).

other good ; by the latter *bonum perfectissimum*, a good which is not only good in its own right, but cannot be regarded as an element in any good greater than itself. Now Virtue or Moral Goodness is, in Kant's judgement, correctly described as *Summum Bonum* in the former, but not in the latter sense. It is good in itself ; its goodness is not dependent on that of anything else to which it is the means, and apart from its success in securing which we should not value it. But it is not the *whole* Good ; for that is Virtue crowned with Happiness ; not Happiness without Virtue, or even barely coinciding, as it were, with Virtue ; but Happiness on the condition of Virtue. Our moral sentiment is offended by the spectacle of Happiness without Virtue in beings capable of Virtue ; and, although the excellence of Virtue is not diminished by dissociation from Happiness, as is that of Happiness by dissociation from Virtue, yet, since it is our duty to produce, so far as in us lies, the best state of the world, our will to perform this, which is our duty, is frustrated if the desire of Happiness inalienable from our nature remain unfulfilled even although we *deserve* that which we desire. Hence, according to Kant, it follows that our moral consciousness must *postulate* a power adequate to bringing the *Summum Bonum* into being—that is, it must postulate the existence of God.

The ' moral ' argument for the existence of God as a Postulate of Practical Reason, which Kant here offers as a substitute for the speculative arguments which he had undermined in his *Critique of Pure Reason*, is exposed to attack on two grounds : (*a*) that of *inconsistency* with his own ethical standpoint, and (*b*) that of *artificiality*.

(*a*) What, it may be asked, has become of the boasted disinterestedness of Kant's ethics, whereby they are supposed to be so remarkably distinguished from all and every form of Eudaemonism, if they be held to postulate a Being willing and able to award Happiness to Virtue, and a capacity in ourselves to participate in the enjoyment of that award ? On this point, however, I think that Kant has an adequate reply. He never fails to insist that any such award of Happiness to Virtue can never serve as a motive to duty without rendering the volition which is thus motived totally destitute of moral value ; but it appears to him unquestionable that, when the conception of a world in which Happiness is awarded to Virtue is presented to the mind—and this ' Reason points out ' (to quote his own words) ' to all rational beings as the goal of all their moral wishes ',[1]—it becomes our duty to promote that Highest Good ; and, since we cannot be bound to do what is impossible, the possibility of this Highest Good is thus *postulated*. Now this implies for Kant both that Virtue can be properly attained (which involves the immortality of the soul) and that there is a Being with the power and will to crown that Virtue with Happiness. Readers of Plato's *Republic* will recall the passages[2] in which it is agreed to

---

[1] *Kr. der pr. V.* (H. v. 121).   [2] ii. 367, iv. 444, 5, x. 612.

inquire whether Justice is or is not to our advantage, apart altogether from the expectation of any rewards, whether in this life or in the next ; and in which, when at last, but only after Justice has been ascertained to be ' the health of the soul ', the question of its advantageousness has answered itself, the rewards are restored to it and the ultimate supremacy of the Good in the universe invoked in support of the belief in an immortal life for the soul, wherein the issues of life are worked out according to a just law. I do not think that there can be denied to be a demand made, as it were, by the moral consciousness upon the world, which is quite distinct from a desire for personal happiness, apart from the hope of attaining which one would not count it worth while to be good ; as may be proved by this claim being quite compatible with an acceptance as just by an individual of his own exclusion, as undeserving, from the happiness which he yet demands that those who deserve it shall attain. Thus I do not hold that the Kantian doctrine of the *Summum Bonum*, which forms the transition in the *Critique of Practical Reason* from Ethics to Religion, can be fairly described as a relapse from the disinterestedness of his ethical teaching into Eudaemonism. We will now turn to the second criticism levelled against this doctrine, which censures it on the score of its artificiality.

(*b*) Unquestionably, as stated, the argument is artificial. It presents the existence of God as merely inferred to account for what is itself neither an

observed fact nor, in its own right, if I may so
express it, a necessary truth of reason, but merely
a presupposition without which a course of action,
in which we nevertheless could not but regard it as
our duty to engage, would seem to be in danger of
frustration. One may say of so roundabout an
argument, with more justice, what Hume said [1] of
Berkeley's in support of his denial of the existence
of unperceived matter, that ' it produces no conviction '; and it certainly is in no way calculated to
express the religious man's conviction of the reality of
the object of his worship ; we shall moreover see later
that Kant appears to have himself become in after
years dissatisfied with it. But it may notwithstanding
be allowed that, if we do not attend so much to the
form which Kant gave to it as to the thought which
seems to underlie it, it does give expression to a real
difficulty which we have in reconciling the imperative urgency of the claim made by the moral law
upon our allegiance with acquiescence in the conviction that the universe is ordered on principles
which are completely indifferent to that law's
demands ; that the voice of conscience, for all its
tone of irresistible authority, is after all only a ' voice
crying in the wilderness ' of an alien world, with the
control of which it has nothing to do, instead of
being, as we were once taught, the voice of One
who was that world's Maker and is still its Governor.

It is then, in fact, by a train of reflection very
similar in substance, though very unlike in form, to

[1] *Enquiry*, § 12 n. (N).

that which is to be found in Bishop Butler's *Sermons upon Human Nature* that Kant, in the *Critique of Practical Reason*, effects a passage from Morality to Religion, or rather from Ethics to Theology. It was the disproportion between the ' manifest authority ' of the law revealed in conscience and the very restricted power which it actually exercises over the world—the world which, says Butler, ' had it power as it had manifest authority, it would absolutely govern,' [1]—that impelled Kant to seek salvation from such mere unreason in faith in an authority, coincident with, or rather identical with, that of conscience, disposing of that power which would seem to be its natural accompaniment, but from which in ourselves it is found divorced.

In any case it is by this road that Kant, as we have seen, effects in the *Critique of Practical Reason* a passage from Ethics to Theology, from the science of Morality to the science of Religion. He defines Religion, as he afterwards continued to define it, as ' the recognition of all duties as divine commands ' ; [2] but he is careful to explain—and this is an essential feature of his view—that these commands must not be regarded in the sense of arbitrary ordinances, imposed by a will quite external to our own, which, so far as we can see, might have been quite opposite to what, as a matter of fact, we find them to be. On the contrary, they are laws which our conscience recognizes as obligatory on every free will ; and thus—there is nothing more essential to Kant's

[1] *Sermon* II. [2] *Kr. der pr. V.* (H. v. 135).

philosophy of religion than this—it is only because a duty is perceived by us to be such on its own account that we are justified in regarding it as commanded by God ; we cannot in any other way become aware that God has commanded something, which would thus become for us a duty merely because so commanded.

He also, in this same treatise, insists, and this too is characteristic, that it is the *moral* attributes of God alone that are of genuinely religious interest—'they include all,' he says, 'in virtue whereof God becomes the object of Religion '.[1] The so-called 'metaphysical ' perfections are ascribed to God only because they are involved in or implied by these moral attributes. Thus Kant here—and it is just this that renders his philosophy of religion epoch-making—definitely denies that the knowledge of God, the Object of religion, falls primarily or properly within the sphere of Physics or of Metaphysics. It is only, according to him, to be reached by starting from the data of ' Practical Reason ', that is, from the consciousness of duty or moral obligation. This doctrine is indeed not without points of contact with the view, common long before Kant among rationalists, both medieval and modern, that Religion has a *merely* practical significance and is concerned not with the greatest possible knowledge that we can attain of ultimate reality, but solely with the best possible conduct of our everyday life, social and individual. But it differs from this view, as

[1] *Kr. der pr. V.* (H. v. 137 n.).

usually held by its supporters, in virtue of Kant's assertion of the *primacy* of Practical Reason, which led him to regard the faith in God which our moral experience suggests to us as, although incapable of developing into speculative or scientific knowledge, nevertheless carrying us, if I may so express it, farther into the heart of reality than the purely speculative or scientific reason could ever take us.

We may also note in passing the account which Kant gives in the *Critique of Practical Reason* [1] of the moral attributes of God, which (as we have just seen) he regards as determining the metaphysical attributes which we may assign to him. These moral attributes are holiness, blessedness, wisdom ; all of which, he observes, imply the absence of limitation ; and form the basis of the triple conception of him as the holy Lawgiver or Creator, the gracious Ruler and Upholder, and the righteous Judge; a trinity in which we shall find him hereafter discovering a correspondence with the traditional Christian conception of the three Persons in the unity of the Godhead.

Ten years after the publication of the *Critique of Practical Reason* appeared, in 1790, the third of Kant's Critiques ; which has by some, not without good reason, been considered his crowning work. This was the *Kritik der Urtheilskraft* or *Critique of the Faculty of Judgement*.[2] This treatise exhibits, in a remarkable degree, Kant's characteristic weakness, his passion for an artificial ' architectonic '. The very title illustrates it. His double interest, to which

[1] Ibid.   [2] H. v. 171 foll.

I have already called attention, in Science on the one hand, in Morality on the other, and his profound sense of their disparateness are reflected in the grand distinction of Speculative and Practical Reason, each with its appropriate 'Critique', devoted to the investigation of the nature and limitations of these two faculties respectively. But there then appear to have forced themselves upon the mind of Kant the problems presented by certain experiences which could not readily be brought under either head, and seemed to suggest some mediation between the 'mighty opposites'; for so we may call the Speculative Reason with its doctrine of universal necessity and the Practical Reason with its postulate of freedom. There was in the first place the problem of *aesthetic taste*, where a judgement not generic but wholly individual—for such a judgement as 'all roses are beautiful' is a mere summation of judgements on individual roses; we can discover no general law requiring roses as such to be beautiful—nevertheless claims universal validity in respect of the pleasure which its object inspires. Here we seem to be in a region midway between that of perception, to which the understanding prescribes laws, and that of desire, to which is addressed the law of conscience; for we can only desire what somehow pleases us, and we can only take pleasure in what we perceive.

And, in the second place, there was the problem of *teleology*, of the determination of the nature of things by their purpose, in which once more we seem to be linking necessity with freedom, and explaining a necessary connexion by a free volition ; a problem thrust into the foreground by the consideration of organic nature, which we seem unable to explain except by using the conception of purpose. Here of course Darwin's procedure confirms Kant, because, even though ' natural selection ' seems often to dispense with purpose, it can only itself be traced by asking ' Of what use is this or that to the organism ? ' This problem of teleology is again akin to the problem of beauty, because in beautiful things we seem to divine significance or meaning. They are no longer like Peter Bell's yellow primrose, that and ' nothing more '; but can ' give ' to us, as the poet who told us of Peter Bell has said, ' thoughts that do often lie too deep for tears '; yet we cannot say *what* the significance or meaning is that we find in them ; it is *Zweckmässigkeit ohne Zweck*, purposiveness without an (external or separable) purpose.

And so Kant classes these problems, which seem to fall between the spheres of the Understanding and of the Reason, of the Speculative and of the Practical Reason, of Necessity and of Freedom, under what he calls the *Urtheilskraft*, the Faculty of Judgement, by which we subsume facts of perception and experience under principles of reason. This is not the place in which further to discuss or to criticize this nomenclature ; but it certainly illustrates that passion of Kant for artificial ' architectonic ' which has been mentioned, and which is responsible for a good deal of what may appear to the reader to be unnecessary repetition in the book itself, due to the supposed obligation laid upon the author to fit his matter into the scheme which he had come to think requisite in a ' Critique '.

On the other hand, it is in the *Kritik der Urtheilskraft* that Kant most conspicuously reaches out, as it were, beyond the negations and contrasts and sharp distinctions upon which he was so apt to dwell, towards a more concrete view of the world, in which, whether through the mediation of the sense of beauty (to the study of which the first part of the book is devoted) or of the immanent purposiveness distinguishing an organism from a machine (to the consideration of which he turns in the second part), a hint is given of a possible reconciliation of what *is* with what *ought to be*, of determinism with liberty. We have already noted that the appearance of design in nature which is most unmistakable in organisms was ever with Kant, even when he is most critical of arguments built upon it, a witness to God ; we shall not therefore be surprised to find in the *Kritik der Urtheilskraft*, and especially in the second part of it, which deals with teleology, passages of great importance to the student of his philosophy of religion.

In the earlier works of Kant we certainly feel that for him ' design in nature ' is generally envisaged as the action of an external artificer moulding a matter or ordering the behaviour of beings which are represented, at least, as though their existence was presupposed by this activity directed upon them.

It was indeed, as we noted, one of his principal criticisms upon the traditional Argument from Design that, except it were eked out by other arguments, it could only, even were it acquitted of all fallacy in its procedure, establish the existence of one or more intelligent architects or manipulators of an independent material, not a God, in the full meaning which that word bears to a monotheist. But in the *Kritik der Urtheilskraft* ' design ' tends to lose this external character. ' One says ', we find Kant remarking, ' far too little of Nature and of the faculty exhibited in its organized productions, if one calls it an analogue of Art (*Analogon der Kunst*); for this implies the thought of the artificer, a rational being, external to it. Rather does it organize itself ; and that, in every species of its organized productions, according indeed to one pattern on the whole, but yet, at the same time, with suitable deviations from it, which the self-preservation of the individual organism demands under the circumstances.'[1]

I suppose Kant to be thinking here of such an instance as is recorded by an observer[2] to have on one occasion overwhelmed him with a sense of a divine wisdom unmistakably guiding the behaviour of the lower creation ; the instance of a pair of swallows in a hard winter throwing out of the nest the young that they could not feed. For here there was a deviation from the general instinct to tend

[1] *Kr. der Urth.*, § 65 ; H. v. 387.
[2] Wasianski, *Kant in seinen letzten Lebensjahren*, p. 192 f. (quoted by Adickes, *Kants Opus Postumum*, p. 829).

the offspring when it was necessary, if all were not to perish, to sacrifice some in the interest of the rest.

Kant goes on : ' One comes nearer perhaps to a true description of this inscrutable property of Nature, if one calls it an analogue of Life (*Analogon des Lebens*).' He points out however that this does not take us far in the understanding of the facts ; for, if we suppose matter itself to be the organizing agent, we seem to invest matter with a property contradictory to its nature ; while, if we suppose the agent to be a soul connected with the body concerned, we are not any nearer the kind of explanation which we desire in the sciences. This cautious recognition of the ambiguous and mysterious character of the conception of Life, which is perhaps too often supposed to enable us to dispense with the need of explaining the apparent presence of intelligence found where we can scarcely attribute it to the individual organism whose behaviour seems to exhibit it, is characteristic of Kant and, I think, worthy of imitation. At the same time it shows that he was alive to that difference of natural processes from the operations of art, our keen perception of which to-day makes the old teleology which is content, with Paley, to compare an organic body to a watch, and hence infer a watchmaker, seem so strangely remote and unconvincing to a generation full of its discovery that operations which consciousness would make intelligible to us, as being like what we know best, namely our own deliberate actions, are often as a matter of fact performed where we have no reason to suppose consciousness present, but rather the contrary.

But it was indeed just because he was deeply impressed by the great difference between an organism and a machine that Kant was always profoundly convinced of the impossibility of the human intelligence explaining the origin of the former on merely mechanical principles, without the use of the conception of purpose. He often expresses this conviction, and in the *Kritik der Urtheilskraft* emphatically denies that we can indulge the hope that a Newton will arise ' to make intelligible ', as he puts it, ' the production of even a single blade of grass by natural laws ordered by no design '.[1] Yet he characteristically refuses to affirm the impossibility that it might be so produced ; lest he should sin against the general principles of his Critical Philosophy by turning what is haply only a limitation of our own faculties into a revelation of the nature of reality as it is in itself. We must not say dogmatically, on the ground of the impossibility of otherwise accounting for the existence of organisms, ' There is a God '; but only, ' We cannot think and make intelligible the purposiveness which we are compelled to consider as presupposed by our knowledge of the inner possibility of many things in Nature except by representing them and the world in general as produced by an intelligent Cause ', that is, by a God.

[1] *Kr. der Urth.*, § 75 ; H. v. 412, 413.

This reduction of our assurance of the existence of God from the appearances of design in nature to acquiescence in the hypothesis of his existence as the only available principle by which to explain the origin of things which nevertheless may have in fact originated otherwise in some manner by us undiscoverable, might seem at first sight to cut the nerve of religious faith. But justly to estimate its place in Kant's general view of the world we must bear in mind his conception of faith as a sufficient ground for action, though not for demonstration to the theoretical intelligence ; and also his doctrine of the primacy of the practical reason over the theoretical. For these prevented him from regarding the impossibility of a theoretical proof that God existed as any justification for living as though he did not exist. He could ' fear God from the heart ', as he assured his old master Schultz that he did, without requiring or hoping for any such theoretical proof of his existence.

Teleology is indeed, he tells us,[1] no part of Theology, though it may be of great use thereto ; since it has no application except as a *heuristic* principle, a principle of discovery, to be used in our investigation of nature ; it has no power to inform us about the nature of God as he is in himself. At first sight this remark seems to contradict Bacon's saying that Final Causes are ' like a virgin consecrated to God, who bears no children ' ;[2] that is, have a devotional value but no practical use in leading to those ' fruits ',

[1] § 79 : H. v. 429.   [2] *De Augm. Sci.*, iii. 5.

available for the relief of man's estate, for which we look as the test of genuine science. But Kant agrees with Bacon that teleology is no part of Natural Science either ;[1] it does not explain the causation of events in nature, like the mechanical laws formulated by Newton. Upon the whole the two philosophers think in the same way of Final Causes. They may suggest clues for discovery, they certainly lift the mind to God ; but they do not enter into strictly scientific explanation, if by that we mean explanation according to mechanical principles; nor do they reveal to us the secrets of the divine nature as it is in itself.

In an extremely interesting paragraph of the work which we are now considering,[2] Kant anticipates later developments of our knowledge of organic nature. He indicates ' the agreement of so many genera of animals in a certain common pattern which seems to underlie not only their anatomical structure but also the disposition of their other members, where a marvellous simplicity of ground plan has been capable of yielding, through the shortening of one part and the lengthening of another, the involution of this and the evolution of that, the vast variety of species which we find '. This suggests to Kant the possibility of a genetic or evolutionary account of organic nature which would allow a ray of hope to enter our minds that we might after all be able to explain the origin of species by means of those principles of the mechanism of nature,

[1] § 79 ; H. v. 430. [2] § 80 ; H. v. 430 foll.

without which there can be no natural science properly so called.

> ' This analogy of forms, so far as they seem among all their differences to be generated in accordance with one common original type, strengthens the suspicion of an actual relationship existing between them in the way of descent from a common progenitor,[1] by exhibiting the gradual approximation of one genus of animal to another,' from man to the polyp, and thence to mosses and lichens, and at last to raw matter, ' out of which and its potencies, according to mechanical laws, similar to those at work in the production of crystals, there seems to be developed the whole scheme of Nature, which in the case of organized beings so baffles our comprehension, that we believe ourselves compelled to conceive another principle ' (that is, the teleological) ' in order to account for it.'

Yet, notwithstanding this prophetic glance into the future of biology, our philosopher is convinced that, even so, the conception of purpose or design, although it may thus be rendered unnecessary for the explanation of the details of organic nature, cannot be excluded altogether. We must suppose some such purpose present in the last resort in that, however we may describe it, from which this whole process of organic evolution takes its origin ; and pantheistic descriptions thereof, whether in Spinoza or in the less definite theories of other thinkers, while they satisfy one condition of all design, namely the unity of the ground, do nothing to help us to a clear conception of the other condition, which is the

---

[1] *Urmutter*. He is possibly thinking of the earth as the ultimate parent of all living things.

relation of this ground to that which is produced out of it. We have still only one way left to us of making this relation intelligible to our reason ; and that is the way of representing it as the intelligent causality of a designing Mind.

But it is clear to Kant that a theology can only be based upon this kind of consideration, if we are content with a God in respect of whom we are unable to explain *why* we want to go beyond the evidence, as we must, if we are to find in the speculative arguments of Rational Theology anything but a ' regulative idea ', or at best a principle useful in facilitating the discovery of natural phenomena. To explain this, however, we must turn to ' practical ' or ' moral ' considerations, which have so far been ignored.

This point, which Kant makes in a later section of the *Kritik der Urtheilskraft*,[1] is the same with that which it is attempted to enforce in a paper which I contributed to a symposium on ' The Idea of a Transcendent Deity ' published in a volume called *Concepts of Continuity* by the Aristotelian Society in 1924. Here, in dealing with the question, propounded at a philosophical congress, whether the idea of a transcendent Deity is philosophically tenable, I contended that, used as it was by philosophers of the seventeenth and eighteenth centuries, as a principle of physical interpretation or as the last chapter of a metaphysical theory which took no special account of religious experience, it is not

[1] § 85 : H. v. 450 foll.

tenable, and is accordingly disappearing from metaphysics as it has already disappeared from physical science ; and that the thinkers of the period I have mentioned only used it as they did, because they had the idea ready to hand, as the result of a religious experience embedded in the tradition of the culture which they inherited and took for granted. In the words with which Kant concludes this section : [1]

> ' Thus Natural Theology (*Physikotheologie*) is a misunderstood Natural (*physische*) Teleology, only serviceable as a preparation or propaedeutic to theology ; and to this purpose it is only adequate if it summon to its aid a principle of different origin, on which and not on itself it can depend for support.'

It is, he tells us a little farther on,[2] ' moral ' or ' ethical ', not ' physical ' or natural teleology which first affords a real foundation for theology. Such a teleology is based, not on the mere impossibility for our understanding of explaining the structure of organisms except on the hypothesis of design, but on the positive affirmation of the absolute value of the good will, in virtue of his capacity for which— not by any means in respect of his happiness—we may, or must, see in man *as a moral being* the ultimate end, in relation to which significance may be attributed to the whole system or process which culminates in him. Apart from conceptions secretly borrowed from the ethical sphere, a physical or natural teleology could not reach a theology ; it could only reach what Kant calls a *demonology*. That

[1] H. v. 455.   [2] § 86 : H. v. 455 foll.

is to say (so we may interpret his thought in terms which are perhaps not quite such as he would himself have chosen), the attribution of anthropomorphic attributes to the ground of nature has no real justification apart from positive moral and religious experience ; so that a ' theology ' which is based wholly on the desire to explain the phenomena of Nature would easily pass (according to Comte's famous law of the three stages) through Pantheism into Naturalism. It is the moral and religious significance of our thought of God which resists its resolution into a vague ' cosmic emotion '.

The section of the *Kritik der Urtheilskraft* of which I have just been giving an account concludes [1] with a very striking remark on the moral sentiments of thankfulness, obedience, and submission to deserved chastisement, which arise in situations such as occur in the course of our lives, as suggesting a divine Object which is adequate to excite them in us. We are not content in happiness without gratitude to Someone who confers it ; in the times when duty demands self-sacrifice, without recognition of a Lord who claims our loyalty ; in penitence, without submission to a Judge before whom we are responsible. The line of reflection is characteristic of Kant, and yet one in which his anxiety to keep within the bounds of a ' critical ' philosophy hindered him from freely developing in a positive manner, as we may find it developed, for example, in Martineau's works, *Types of Ethical Theory* and *A Study of*

[1] H. v. 459.

Religion, or as the late Professor Cook Wilson might have developed it had he followed up his suggestive paper on 'Rational Grounds of Belief in God', now included in the collection of his Remains posthumously published under the title *Statement and Inference*.[1]

Now, when we think of God in this way as a transcendent Being whose voice is heard in the categorical imperative, as Kant called it, of duty, and whom we can regard as our Creator and our Judge, we are of course soon reminded, if we are students of philosophy, that at least one thinker of the first rank has been an atheist, in the sense that he rejected all theism of this kind, while at the same time he combined with this rejection and the atheism which it may seem to involve, not only a moral elevation of character which, as displayed in his life, compelled the reverence of all who came into contact with him, but, what is more remarkable, a religious passion which has earned him the epithet of God-intoxicated, and has drawn towards him as a kindred soul men to whom the Kantian fear of a dimly descried imponent of the moral law appears scarcely religious at all. I refer, of course, to Spinoza.

As I have already said, the long neglect of Spinoza as an enemy of religion was in Kant's own lifetime drawing to an end. Not only had Goethe, the great poet of the younger generation, expressed in verse thoughts confessedly inspired by him, but, when this verse was shown by Jacobi to Lessing, the man

[1] Part V., §§ 565 foll.

among Kant's contemporaries whose influence on the literature and general intellectual development of his countrymen was most conspicuous, the older man had confessed that for him there was no philosophy but Spinoza's and that, if he should call himself any man's disciple, it would be his.

This being so, a particular interest attaches to an analysis which Kant attempts in the *Kritik der Urtheilskraft* [1] of the state of mind of a ' well-disposed man, such as Spinoza ' (the instance was only added in the second edition) ' who is firmly convinced that there is no God and no future life '.

The following passage does not, I think it must be admitted, display any great comprehension of Spinoza, if we are to take it as intended to apply to him, but it incidentally suggests some valuable thoughts.

' We may thus ', Kant observes, ' suppose a well-disposed man who is firmly convinced that there is no God and (what, in regard to the object of morality, comes to the same thing) no future life either ; how will he judge concerning his own inner determination to an end by means of the moral law, which in practice he reveres ? He demands no advantage to himself from obedience to it, either in this world or in another ; rather does he disinterestedly will merely the establishment of the Good towards which that holy law directs all his faculties. But his striving is limited ; and from Nature he can expect indeed an occasional coincidence, but never a regular conformity according to constant principles with the end which he notwithstanding feels himself bound and impelled to bring about. Deceit, violence, jealousy will

[1] § 87 ; H. v. 466.

always prevail around him, though he himself is honest, peaceable, and benevolent; and the other well-disposed men whom he encounters will, notwithstanding all their deserving to be happy, yet, through the indifference of Nature, be subject to all the evils of want, sickness, and untimely death, like the beasts of the earth, and will so continue until one wide grave swallows them all together (just or unjust, it makes no difference), and casts back them who would believe that they were the final purpose of creation into the abyss of the purposeless chaos of matter whence they were drawn. Thus the end which this well-disposed man had, and was bound to have, before his eyes in following the laws of morality, he must assuredly give up as impossible of attainment; or else, if he wishes to remain still faithful to the moral vocation whereof he is inwardly conscious, and not to suffer the feeling of reverence, inspired in him directly by the Moral Law and urging him to obey it, to be weakened by disbelief in the reality of the only ideal end adequate to its sublime demands— a weakening which cannot but involve damage to the moral sentiment—he must, as he quite well can, since there is nothing essentially contradictory in the assumption, assume, from a practical point of view, that is to say, in order to form for himself at least a conception of the end presented to him as a moral duty, the existence of a Moral Author of the world, that is, of God.'

Spinoza indeed was not at all like the 'well-disposed' atheist of Kant's picture. There was not in his view any such antagonism between the actual world and the ideal presented by conscience as Kant supposes him to feel, and as Kant himself would have felt had he been constrained by irresistible reasons to abandon his faith in God and immortality, instead of only to give up the hope of demonstrating their existence on purely theoretical grounds. The Jewish philosopher could find in the satisfaction of his intelligence by the vision of an unbroken order everywhere, whether in the world of bodies or in the world of thoughts, sufficient to arouse the religious passion which he named the *amor intellectualis Dei* ; on the other hand the moral law was to him not, as to Kant, the supreme or rather the only revelation of God's true nature, but the formulation of the way best calculated to obtain the happiness appropriate to our situation in that eternal universe which is the one and only God, in whom or in which whatever is has its being.

But it is probable that there are many to whom the attitude which Kant attributes to his righteous atheist is more familiar than that which was actually exemplified by the illustrious thinker whom he chose to name as an instance of this character. It is expressed in the story [1] of George Eliot walking with Frederic Myers in the Fellows' garden of Trinity College at Cambridge, talking ' with terrible earnestness ' of God and Duty and Immortality : ' how inconceivable the first, how unbelievable the third, and yet how peremptory and absolute the second'. And I do not think it can be denied that this position is profoundly unsatisfactory, and that it seems to urge any one who finds himself in it to advance to faith in God as required to justify our recognition of the authority of the moral law ; not as though that authority were otherwise than immediately ' manifest ', as Butler expresses it, or needed

[1] Told in Myers's Essay on *George Eliot*.

an external sanction to establish it ; but because, without faith in God, it must seem to be, as I put it before, a voice crying in the wilderness of an alien world, its presence wherein must remain an inexplicable and baffling mystery ; and because this impression, while it does not take away from us our inexpugnable consciousness of the urgency of the claim made by that law upon us, can hardly but tend to discourage us in our moral endeavours and to sap our moral energies, which seem destined to perpetual disappointment in a system of things wholly indifferent to our moral purposes. A problem, of which Kant was acutely conscious, remains however when, as a consequence of faith in God, we allow ourselves to give to morality a place in the system of things which experience might seem to deny it ; the problem namely of keeping morality wholly pure from extraneous motives, such as that of winning divine favour or assuring our personal salvation in another life. It is the primary doctrine of Kant that, while morality suggests and may perhaps even be said to require the representation of its laws as divine commands, and thereby passes into religion, it is essential to the true or truly moral religion that God's will cannot be separated from morality, or ascertained otherwise than through our conscience ; the very essence of idolatry [1] being the supposition that God's will can be done otherwise than by conduct intrinsically good, or his favour won by any other means than by a morally good disposition.

[1] *Kr. der Urth.*, § 89 ; H. v. 473.

V

KANT'S PHILOSOPHY OF RELIGION: 'RELIGION WITHIN THE LIMITS OF MERE REASON'

THE concluding section of the *Kritik der Urtheilskraft* contains much of interest to the student of Kant's philosophy of religion ; but nothing, I think, upon which it is necessary for us now to dwell ; for that part which concerns the relation of positive religion in general, and of Christianity in particular, to natural religion anticipates the teaching of the work on *Religion within the Limits of mere Reason*, which is Kant's principal contribution to the subject, and to the consideration of which we shall shortly be turning. But, before so turning, a few words are called for upon a little treatise which preceded it by two years, *Ueber das Misslingen aller philosophischen Versuche in der Theodicee*,[1] 'On the Miscarriage of all philosophical Attempts at Theodicy ' ; for here too Kant is occupied with theological problems. Written in 1791, in view of the fears excited in conservative bosoms by the French Revolution— which Kant at first welcomed with enthusiasm— and after the accession to the Prussian throne in 1786, in the place of Frederick the Great, of Frederick William II, who was much under the influence of advisers favourable to an obscurantist policy in

[1] H. vi. 75 foll.

matters of religion, it gives the first indication of strained relations between its author and the ecclesiastical authorities. Under the reign of Frederick the Great, himself an open partisan of French ' free thought ', one Von Zedlitz had been Minister of Public Worship and Education, and had devoted himself to the advancement of intellectual freedom and progress in the kingdom. He had especially encouraged and shown respect to Kant, of whose philosophy he was a student and admirer, and with whom he engaged in a personal correspondence. In 1778 he offered the philosopher a post at the University of Halle, better paid than that which he held at Königsberg. Kant declined the offer ; but he afterwards evinced his appreciation of the attention paid him by this enlightened statesman in a striking manner, by honouring him with the dedication of the *Critique of Pure Reason*. Two years after the accession of Frederick William II, Von Zedlitz was dismissed from office and replaced by a certain Wöllner.

Wöllner was an ex-clergyman, who was associated with the pseudo-mystical and politically reactionary movement then fashionable under the name of Rosicrucianism ; and in 1788 he promulgated, with the royal authority, an edict against the current rationalism, threatening all teachers of subjects bearing on religion who should be found unorthodox with removal from their chairs and pulpits. Three years later, in 1791, the date of the essay with which I am now concerned, a commission of three members was established, with very extensive powers of censorship, to test the doctrines of all instructors, in schools and universities as well as in parish churches.

It was, no doubt, in view of this movement that Kant published the treatise in question. In it he indicated the chief difficulties which attempts at theodicy, at a justification of the ways of God to man, have to meet ; difficulties arising from the existence of pain or of moral evil, and of the un-deserved sufferings of the good ; and the inadequacy of all the solutions commonly suggested. He pointed to the hero of the Book of Job as an example of the right attitude to be taken up in the situation ; an attitude of resolute refusal to ' lie for God ', while preserving a practical faith in divine justice, based not upon reasoning but upon the conviction that it is our duty to live in accordance with the dictates of conscience, however dark the outlook ; and added that, had Job appeared before any tribunal of dogmatic theologians, any synod, inquisition, vener-able *classis*, or high consistory (*Oberconsistorium*) of the present day—one only excepted—he would have met with a lamentable fate.[1]

This mention of ' one only exception ' I take to be an ironical reference to the new inquisitorial commission, which bore this very title of *Ober-consistorium*. It did not, however, venture at once on direct measures against Kant, although, as a correspondent at Berlin privately informed him, one

[1] H. vi. 89.

N

of its members, a certain Woltersdorf, pastor of Trinity Church in Berlin, had his eye upon him, and had even proposed to the king that he should be forbidden to write any further on subjects which touched upon religion. This new tract was itself not calculated to conciliate those who were already suspicious of the tendency of his teaching to unsettle the orthodoxy of his students. He makes it clear that he will have nothing to do with a relapse from the recognition of the moral law written in our hearts as the sole expression of the divine will for us into pious reflections on the difference between God's ways and ours. No one, he declares, with the slightest feeling for morality could entertain the plea *Sunt superis sua jura* ('the gods have their own code') as a satisfactory defence of God against the impeachment of his justice on the score of the evils in the world.[1] Nor does he fail to point out the essential weakness of the familiar argument that from the injustice of this life one can reason to the justice to be expected in another ; namely that we here infer that the part of God's ways which we do not see will be—not like but—unlike the only part which we do see.[2] He will not in fine allow that any scientific theodicy is possible. We are dealing with a ' matter of *faith* ' (*eine Glaubenssache*). But he is careful to distinguish such a ' *matter* of faith ' from an ' *article* of faith ' (*Glaubenssatz, Glaubensartikel*) ; and, in a vigorous appendix,[3] denounces

[1] H. vi. 80.   [2] H. vi. 84.

[3] H. vi. 91 ; cp. *Rel. innerh. der Gr. der bl. V.*, H. vi. 286.

all use of creeds as tests, exposing the great temptation which it must always offer to insincerity, especially where a man's livelihood depends upon his subscription. It is, however, fair in this connexion to observe that it is recorded of the few cases in which a clergyman was deprived of his benefice by the activities of the commission set up by Wöllner, that Frederick William ordered such persons to be provided with a well-paid secular post instead.

At this juncture it was probably with some satisfaction at the opportunity which it would give him of delivering his conscience from any fear that he was by his silence deceiving others as to his true convictions that Kant set about the publication of his thoughts on religion by issuing in the journal called the *Berliner Monatschrift* an essay on the Radical Evil in Human Nature, which was eventually to constitute the first section of his great work on the philosophy of religion. Although this Review was printed at Jena, Kant expressly desired the publisher to submit his contribution to the new tribunal at Berlin ; where one of the three censors, a certain Hillmer, passed it with the remark that ' it might be printed, since only profound scholars read Kant '. But when the second section, ' On the Conflict of the Good Principles with the Evil for the Supremacy over Mankind ' was similarly submitted, Hillmer thought that Kant was not confining himself to purely philosophical considerations, but ' trenching on biblical theology ' ; and, calling in his colleague Hermes, refused the *imprimatur*, declining to give the publisher of the Review in which it was to have appeared any reasons for his refusal beyond a general reference to the *Religions-edict* of Frederick William II already mentioned.

Kant did not, however, accept this rebuff as final ; and, on his submitting the section thus censured, together with the two following, which were to complete his examination of the philosophical basis of religion—one dealing with the Victory of the Good Principle, and one with True and False Worship under the Supremacy of the Good Principle —to the examination of the theological faculty of his own University, it was, as one would expect, passed by his colleagues thereon ; and at Easter 1793 appeared the entire work under the title ' Religion within the Limits of mere Reason ' (*Religion innerhalb der Grenzen der blosen Vernunft*).[1]

The first section of this work deals, as I have already said, with the ' radical evil ' in human nature. This is the profoundest and most original portion of the whole, and we may rightly call it epoch-making ; for it terminates in this department of thought the period of self-styled *Aufklärung* or Enlightenment, to which no ancient doctrine of the Christian Church was more uncongenial than that of Original Sin, a doctrine which Kant here revives, not as a revealed dogma, but as an implication of our moral experience, making it the foundation of

---

[1] H. vi. 95 foll.

his whole theory of the nature and function of religion in human life.

Kant begins by contrasting the old and widely spread belief in a golden age from which we have degenerated with the more modern and less widely spread notion, ' found only among philosophers and in our times chiefly among pedagogues ',[1] of the world as progressing from bad to better. If by this be meant, not progress in culture or civilization, which Kant would not deny, but genuinely moral progress, the belief in it is not, he remarks,[2] founded on experience ; and he suggests that it is rather a kindly supposition, by which moralists, from Seneca to Rousseau, have designed to encourage us to develop the germ of goodness that our nature contains. He proposes an intermediate view between that which sees in man's original nature something merely evil, and one which sees in it something wholly good ; a view according to which good and evil are both present therein. But he cannot acquiesce in such a view, which would imply that the moral law requires of us less than an absolute obedience. One who is a moral being at all, capable of either moral goodness or moral evil, if not by nature good must be by nature bad. And thus man, who is found by experience everywhere to fall short of the demand of the law, may be called by nature bad. Kant does not however teach, as some have done, the total depravity of human nature. A susceptibility to good, such as is implied in the very

[1] H. vi. 113.   [2] H. vi. 114.

consciousness of duty, must indeed be assumed to make an action morally bad ; and the existence in man of good dispositions, capable of training and development, Kant expressly and readily affirms.[1]

We are not, so Kant insists,[2] to regard the evil in us as a mere negation of goodness. For the very nature of moral goodness consists in the activity of the law as the spring or motive power of our will. When the law is thus present to us, it must move our will to action in accordance with it, but for a positive bad principle leading to disobedience.

An act done without perception of our obligation to do otherwise would not be bad. As St. Paul says :[3] ' I had not known sin, but by the law.' A really ' indifferent ' act would be, according to Kant's usual phraseology, an act of *nature*, not of *freedom*, and so would not enter into the sphere of morality at all. Kant explains [4] that when, as in this section of the book we are now studying, we raise the question whether by nature a man is good or bad or partly good and partly bad, we are not conforming to that phraseology. We are inquiring after what he calls the subjective ground of our use of freedom in general, which precedes any act which is perceptible by the senses. This cannot be, in the strict sense, a *natural* fact determining the will, but must be a rule made by the will for itself, that is, in Kant's technical language, a *maxim*.

It must be borne in mind that by a *maxim* Kant always, in his ethical writings, means what he calls

[1] H. vi. 120.   [2] H. vi. 116 n.   [3] Rom. vii. 7.   [4] H. vi. 115.

' a subjective spring ' of action—that is to say, that which actually determines in will in some particular case. The origin of this use of the word is to be explained as follows. Every properly human—that is, deliberately willed—act is done for some *reason*, subsumed, as it were in a syllogism, under some general major premise or *major propositio*. That to which in any individual case an act is ultimately referred is thus the ultimate major premise, *maxima propositio* or *maxim*. This may be one's duty, or it may be one's own pleasure ; either may serve as a *maxim*, but only the former is the *law*, which *ought* to determine our action ; and hence the man who wills aright, doing all that he does because it is his duty, has adopted the law into his maxim.

By insisting [1] that no actions, properly so called— that is, voluntary actions—can be really *adiaphora*, morally indifferent, no characters that are really neither good nor evil, Kant placed himself deliber- ately, as he himself remarks, on the side of the ' rigorists ' against the ' latitudinarians '. I have already called attention, in a different connexion, to this feature of his ethical doctrine ; for it is this sharp opposition of good and evil, this division of the field between them, that indisposes him to conceive of moral improvement as a gradual passage from worse to better, and makes him see a truer con- ception of it in such a notion of *conversion* as must have been familiar to him from his Pietistic training,

[1] H. vi. 116.

than in the establishment of a harmonious mean, as suggested in Aristotle's *Ethics*. With this preference went in him, not unnaturally, though perhaps not necessarily, a tendency to express himself as though the sense of duty excluded any emotional satisfaction in its performance, so that the presence of anything of the kind must mar its purity.

There is a well-known epigram of the poet Schiller (who was a great admirer of Kant, but could not resist the temptation to caricature this tendency), in which he spoke of ' now being sure at last that one is doing one's duty, when one does it with aversion '.[1] In an essay on ' Grace and Dignity in Morality ', published after the separate appearance of the Kantian treatise on Radical Evil, he criticized Kant's rigorism and said that ' Even in the purest manifestations of the divine part of his nature, man must not leave the sensuous behind ; he must not found the triumph of the one on the suppression of the other. Only when it flows from his entire humanity as the result of the united action of both principles, when it has become second nature to him, is his morality secure.'[2] It was inevitable that the austerity of Kant's representation of morality should give pause to a poet, however susceptible to the poetic quality of its very austerity ; and Kant's revulsion from the Aristotelian tradition to an enthusiast for Hellenic culture.

[1] *Werke*, i. 268 (ed. 1904).
[2] Ibid., xi. (ed. 1904). Quoted by Höffding, *History of Modern Philosophy*, Eng. tr., ii. 131.

His criticism did not escape Kant's attention; and there appeared in the completed work the following note [1] appended to the passage we are now discussing; a note so important for understanding Kant's attitude in this matter and so significant for his position with regard to Religion—in which (as Matthew Arnold's famous definition [2] reminds us) morality is ' touched by emotion '—that I do not hesitate to quote it at length.

' Professor Schiller,' says Kant, ' in his masterly essay on " Grace and Dignity in Morality ", finds fault with this manner of representing Obligation, as though it implied a Carthusian [3] temper : but I cannot, as he and I are at one in the most important principles, admit here either any disagreement; if only we can make ourselves intelligible to one another. I readily allow that I cannot, just because of its *dignity*, associate with the conception of Duty any *grace*.[4] For the conception of Duty implies an unconditional constraint, wherewith *grace* stands in direct contradiction. The majesty of the law (as of that given on Sinai) inspires awe (not fear which repels, nor attraction which invites to familiarity, but awe), which arouses reverence on the part of the recipients of its commands towards the giver of them ; and when, as in the present case, this lawgiver is within ourselves, a feeling of the sublimity of our own destiny, which attracts us more than any beauty. But Virtue, that is to say the firmly established disposition to fulfil one's duty adequately, is in its consequences also beneficent, beyond anything

[1] H. vi. 117.   [2] *Literature and Dogma*, ed. 1883, p. 16.
[3] i. e. ascetic.

[4] The word used is *Anmuth*, which presumably implies *pleasantness* more than our word *grace* does.

that Nature or Art can accomplish ; and the glorious picture of Humanity exhibited in this form admits very well of the companionship of the Graces, who yet, when there is still question of Duty alone, keep themselves at a respectful distance. Only after his conquest of the monsters does Hercules become the leader of the Muses ; before that labour, while it is going on, the good sisters shrink back. These attendants of Venus Urania are but courtesans in the train of Venus Dione, so soon as they interfere in the business of Duty, and desire to supply motives thereto. Now, if one asks of what sort is the aesthetic condition and temperament of Virtue, whether spirited and cheerful, or anxious and dejected, it is hardly necessary to give the obvious reply. The latter slavish temper cannot be present without a secret hatred of the law, and cheerfulness of heart in the discharge of one's duty, which must be distinguished from complacency in the recognition of it, is a sign of the genuineness of a virtuous sentiment, even in the case of piety, which consists not in the self-tormenting of the penitent sinner— for this is highly ambiguous, and is commonly only an inward self-reproach for having offended against the rules of prudence—but rather in the firm purpose to do better in future ; which, when cheered by good progress, must produce a cheerful temper, apart from which one is never certain that one has fallen in love with goodness, or in other words, adopted it into one's maxim '—

that is to say, made it the principle of one's actions.

Such is Kant's considered judgement upon the charge, which Schiller has by no means been the last critic to bring against his ethics, of ignoring the pleasures of virtue and the beauty of holiness, and representing Duty under an aspect of repellent

and unlovely austerity. I think that he shows satisfactorily that the good man need not dislike his
duty, and even that delight in doing it, so long as
he does not do it in order to please himself thereby,
is, as Aristotle had long ago said,[1] a sign that a good
habit has been formed, and so a test of virtue. But
it remains obvious that the mood which we associate
with some of the greatest saints—the mood of
' rejoicing in spirit ', ' rejoicing in the Lord ', and
the like—was one to which Kant was on the whole
a stranger. I translated above ' *das Gut auch lieb
gewonnen* ' by ' fallen in love with goodness ', but
I doubt whether the German is really so strong,
and would not be more closely rendered as ' conceived a liking or affection for goodness '. The
argument will, however, bear the stronger phrase ;
and we need to be able to use it, if we are to have
an ethics which can find room for some of the
highest experiences of the human spirit.

We must now return to the main course of Kant's
argument. We have already noted that he admits [2]
a capacity for good in man. Indeed the propensity
to evil which he discovers in us could not be imputed
to us, did we not conceive it as presupposing a state
of innocence from which we have fallen ; and not
only so—for the most extreme doctrine of human
depravity does as much as this—but the deeds which
proceed from our propensity to evil would not be
morally imputable, did we not still retain our free-

[1] *Eth. Nic.* ii. 3. 1104 b. 4 foll.
[2] H. vi. 120 ff.

dom to obey the law, from obedience to which that propensity diverts us. Our animal, our human or rational, and our personal or responsible capacities are all in themselves blameless or good. But there is also in us a propensity to evil, which manifests itself in three degrees ; as *frailty*, expressed in the Pauline complaint : ' To will is present with me, but how to perform I find not ' ;[1] as *impurity of motive*, which requires other determinants of our will, beside the law itself, to make us obey it ; finally, as *depravity*, the preference of other motives to that of duty. The man whose conduct is conformed to the law, *bene moratus*, may not be *moraliter bonus*, morally good, in the proper sense of the words. The man who is merely *bene moratus* does not differ outwardly from him who is *moraliter bonus*, yet the obedience of the one is in the letter, the latter in the spirit ; and only the latter has the character of goodness ; as St. Paul said, ' Whatsoever is not of faith is sin '.[2]   This text Kant interprets[3] of all actions that do not proceed from the principle of duty *alone* ; and we commonly assume in every man a propensity to act otherwise than thus. But such a propensity cannot have the character of moral evil unless it be our own act ; and so if, as is the case, we cannot trace the beginning of our propensity to evil to any individual act of our own, and at the same time cannot ascribe it to a merely *natural* defect (which would take away its moral character altogether), we have to distinguish what

[1] Rom. vii. 18.   [2] Rom. xiv. 23.   [3] H. vi. 124.

Kant calls[1] an *intelligible* act not in time, the *original sin* of the theologians, from an *empirical* or *phenomenal* act in time, which is only a derivative sin, presupposing that which we call *original* as its root. ' The former ', says Kant,[2] ' is, compared with the latter, a mere propensity, and moreover innate, both because it cannot be eradicated—since, to eradicate it, the highest maxim ' (that is, the actual spring of action) ' would have to be that of the Good ; whereas, in speaking of this propensity to evil, we assume it to be bad ;—and also especially for the reason that we can as little assign a cause why in us Evil has corrupted our highest or ultimate maxim (although this is our own act) as we can assign a cause of any fundamental propensity of our nature.'

This unquestionably very difficult conception is the corner-stone of Kant's theory of the Fall and Atonement, as we may describe, using traditional language, the theological doctrine expounded in the book before us ; and we must fix it in our minds if we are to make anything of his philosophy of religion.

Perhaps the most convenient way of doing this will be to contrast it with the views most inconsistent with it ; on the one side with the view which sees in the propensity of our nature to what we now regard as evil nothing but our inheritance of animal instincts, innocent in our sub-human ancestors, but out of keeping with our present environment—the ' ape and tiger ' in us which are long a-dying ; and

[1] H. vi. 125.   [2] H. vi. 126.

on the other side with a view probably more often entertained in the period of the *Aufklärung* which closes in Kant than in our own time, obsessed as we are with the thought of inherited disadvantages and unconscious motives—the view which regards every child of man as born good, and only perverted by his own individual fault or by the misfortune of his individual education. The latter of these two views does not in Kant's opinion harmonize with the facts of experience—with the universal prevalence of sin and our common assumption of its presence in every man. The former contradicts our sense of responsibility for what we yet cannot trace to an origin within our own individual lives. Better, Kant thinks, to confess to something in the situation which baffles our understanding than to tamper with our moral consciousness (which is to him the primary certainty in our experience) by denying our responsibility as free agents, or to give the lie to patent facts by disputing the existence of a propensity to evil in man to which all history and all experience testify.

It is necessary here, in Kant's judgement, to allege the testimony of history and experience, because .the propensity of evil in human nature cannot be deduced from the conception of humanity ; if it could, it would imply that man was not free in his choice of evil, and thus his choice of it could not be imputed to him as something for which he is morally responsible. This view of Kant's is opposed to the derivation (which we may perhaps call Hegelian) of original sin in man from his *finitude* ;

for finitude would certainly seem to be an essential part of the conception of humanity, so that, if sin were necessarily connected therewith, we could deduce its presence in all men from that conception. No doubt there are thinkers who would in one sense deny finitude to be part of the conception of humanity, in that they would hold the essential difference between humanity and a merely animal nature to lie precisely in the self-conscious presence in humanity of the infinite or divine nature. But they would, I suppose, conceive what has been called ' original sin ' in man to be incidental to the manifestation of the infinite or divine nature in a finite form ; whether or no they would admit any divine life to be conceivable which did not so manifest itself. As we shall see, when we come to deal with the *Opus postumum*, there is a tendency in Kant's thinking which might have led him in this direction ; but he did not habitually think in this manner. It is characteristic of him that he speaks [1] of man as neither beast nor devil ; Aristotle [2] had spoken of him as neither beast nor god. Kant's conception of humanity was that of a union of rational nature with animal sensibility ; and this does not, he thinks, in itself involve a propensity to evil. But experience does not permit us to deny that such a propensity is always and everywhere found in man.

Kant marshals the evidence of its existence—from the cruelty of savages, from the vices of the civilized,

[1] H. vi. 131. [2] *Pol.* i. 2. 1253 a. 29.

from the mutual hostility of States.[1] What is the cause, he asks, of this universal depravity ? It is not our animal sensibility ; for that affords goodness its opportunity no less than badness ; and we are not responsible for that, as we are for the evil actions of which we are thinking. Nor is it a corruption of our moral reason, for this is not corrupted ; were it corrupted, we should be devils, not men, making antagonism to the law our maxim— as Milton's Satan is represented as doing, when he exclaims ' Evil, be thou my good ! ' [2] But the maxim which is the motive of our undutiful actions is not this ; it is the principle of self-love, which is inseparably associated with our physical sensuous nature. The difference between moral goodness and moral badness lies in the subordination of the principle of duty to that of self-love ; and thus we must reckon as a bad man not only him who gratifies his selfish inclinations to the neglect of his duty, but also him who does that which it is his duty to do as a means to his own happiness. He alone is a good man who only seeks to *deserve* happiness by obedience to the moral law ; although we may be unable to distinguish from his genuine worth the character of the seemingly dutiful man whom mere absence of temptation or of opportunity keeps in the path of virtue. But if, as the English cynic declared, every man has his price ; if there is really, as some would assert, and as it would be hard to disprove, no one whom a sufficient inducement would not

[1] H. vi. 127 foll.   [2] *Paradise Lost*, iv. 110.

persuade to abandon that path ; then St. Paul may well have been in the right when he exclaimed : ' There is no difference, for all have sinned ; there is none that doeth good, no, not one.'[1] The true moral judgement thus divides men into good and bad, and admits no intermediate characters, although an empirical survey finds many which we should pronounce neither good nor bad, or partly good and partly bad. But this very fact means that, while the absolute dichotomy of good and bad is apprehended by our reason as the only intelligible distinction, to apply it in experience must be beyond our power.

Whence then the origin of this propensity in us to evil ? With a touch of humour Kant describes [2] the three ways of explaining it which commend themselves to the three higher Faculties of Medicine, Law, and Theology respectively. These are inherited disease (*Erbkrankheit*), inherited guile (*Erbschuld*), inherited sin (*Erbsünde*). This last is the usual German expression for what we call ' original sin ', but, will be observed, introduces the notion of *inheritance*, which is absent from our expression, literally translated as it is from the Augustinian Latin phrase, to which Kant does not object. Kant however will have nothing to do with this notion of *inheritance*. He quotes from Ovid, *Genus et proavos et quae non fecimus ipsi, vix ea nostra puto.*[3] All these ways of regarding our propensity to evil as inherited remove the responsibility of it from ourselves and

---

[1] Rom. iii. 22, 23, 12 ; so quoted H. vi. 133.
[2] H. vi. 133 f.   [3] *Metam.* xiii. 140, 141 ; quoted H. vi. 134.

place it upon our progenitors. It is clear that Kant is not among those who would deny that ' original sin ' can properly be called *sin* at all ; for him it is just the salient fact about the moral consciousness that it imputes to us as sin what we notwithstanding perceive to be presupposed in our first experience of a wrong choice ; and hence, however great the difficulty—should it even prove an impossibility—of understanding how, being thus presupposed, it can be imputed as sin, Kant yet insists that we cannot refuse so to impute it without giving our conscience the lie when it reproaches us for acts of choice which presuppose it ; and we must always remind ourselves that to Kant nothing in heaven or earth is so sure as the witness of conscience to the moral law, of unfaithfulness to which it convicts us.

Every actual sin, indeed, so Kant urges,[1] must be regarded as, in a sense, ' original ' ; for it cannot, without prejudice to its character of a free choice, be considered as *determined* by its antecedents ; it must be regarded as if the sinner had fallen into it directly from the state of innocence. It is a contradiction, he tells us, to seek a temporal origin of free actions as such, as though (in that capacity) they were natural effects. Here of course Kant is thinking of the theory of Freedom which he had already announced in his writings on moral philosophy ;[2] according to which we are constrained by

---

[1] H. vi. 135.

[2] *Grundlegung der Metaphysik der Sitten*, 3. Abschn. ; H. iv. 294 foll.

the nature of our cognitive faculties—since we have no way of perceiving or intuiting, except in space and time—to *perceive* as an act in time (and therefore as determined by its antecedents) what notwithstanding we are compelled, from the point of view of morality, to regard as a wholly free act, which we need not have done. There is here for him no contradiction, since we are not speaking of the same thing in both cases—but, in the one, of a *phenomenon*, in the other of an *intelligible* or *noumenal* fact. Hence the double aspect which is worn by our actions, or rather by the volitions from which they proceed— of events in time, preceded, like all other such events, by an infinite series of other events, from which we cannot but assume that the present action necessarily follows ; and of moral facts, which we impute to ourselves as good or evil, according as they are or are not determined by the law which our conscience recognizes as binding upon us. This double aspect is only a special case of the general antithesis, which runs all through the Kantian philosophy, of *phenomena* or things as they appear and *noumena* or things as they are understood to be.

This doctrine of moral freedom is capable both of an interpretation which denies any real freedom to the individual in his particular actions, and of one which allows him a genuine initiative in each action. The former interpretation is that placed upon it by Schopenhauer, who definitely holds[1] that, Space and Time being unreal appearances, so too is the

[1] *Die Welt als Wille und als Vorstellung*, §§ 23 ff. ; cp. § 70.

individuality of beings spatially and temporally distinct from each other ; that thus the reality in our
actions is an eternal choice of the One Will, whereof
we are all but transient manifestations in space and
time ; and that this eternal choice is free or ground-
less ; but that, as events in time, our actions are no
less determined than all other natural events.

I do not think that Kant would have accepted this
dotting of his i's and crossing of his t's ; but it is
obviously a way in which his doctrine may be interpreted. On the other hand, it is possible to say
that undoubtedly what we call a free act *looks* from
the outside just like any other event in time ; in the
case of other events we by no means always see
how they have necessarily followed from their antecedents, but we take it for granted that they have
so followed and that, with a sufficient knowledge of
the circumstances—which we may not be able to
obtain,—we could see *how* ; and that there is nothing to distinguish human actions, as looked at from
the outside, as *phenomena*, from any other events.
But, we may go on to say, *from within*, from our
sense of remorse when we act in one way, and our
peace of conscience when we act in another, we
know that the act was, as it seemed to us *in doing it*,
a free expression of our own present nature. I think
that this interpretation is truer to Kant's own
thought than that offered by Schopenhauer ; but
Kant himself always insists that there is in our
freedom a real *inscrutability* to the speculative understanding ; when we try to think it out we (as Milton

tells us was the experience of the fallen angels who entertained themselves with the discussion of the problem) ' find no end, in wandering mazes lost '.[1]

I return to the discussion in *Religion within the Limits of Mere Reason*, where Kant is not concerned to expound, but rather assumes, the doctrine of Freedom which we find in his earlier writings on moral philosophy. His object here is to insist on the impossibility of explaining by its antecedents the evil propensity which we discover in ourselves resisting the demands of the moral law, and on the consequent inevitableness of imputing to ourselves the guilt of the rebellious actions which it induces. He now goes on [2] to declare that the story of the Fall in Genesis represents the fact sufficiently well. We fall in Adam, who fell—as, from the intelligible, though not from the empirical or phenomenal point of view, we all fall—from a state of innocence. Yet there is no fundamental corruption of our will, but a propensity of inscrutable origin. For it is represented as coming by way of seduction by a Spirit in whom it existed beforehand.

Kant is of course here taking the usual traditional interpretation and setting of the Fall-story. He is not an Old Testament critic, inquiring after its original significance to those who first told it. Indeed he expressly remarks [3] that he does not decide whether his interpretation gives the actual meaning of the Biblical writer.

The seducer, in whom the propensity to evil is

[1] *Paradise Lost*, ii. 561.　　[2] H. vi. 135 ff.　　[3] H. vi. 137 *n*.

represented as existing beforehand, is the *Devil*, whose will is distinguished from the human as being fundamentally corrupt, and who is therefore incapable of restoration. The evil in the will of such a being is not, like that in the will of human beings, partially explicable by the presence of a fleshly nature which is given an undue precedence over the rational ; its source is to us utterly inexplicable and inscrutable.

An *historical* explanation of the origin of the evil propensity in man Kant of course could not accept, as our previous account of his teaching has abundantly shown. *Original* sin is not for him *inherited* sin. We cannot seriously regard Adam's sin as affecting us through physical descent, juridical succession, or implication in the results of his rebellion against God. He stands for each of us. *Mutato nomine, de te fabula narratur.*[1] We *all* fall as he is asserted to have fallen. He is, so to say, ' Everyman '. We too are tempted. We are tempted, like him, through our sensual appetites ; and this affords us a hope of recovery which we could not have, did we not with an uncorrupted reason recognize the obligation to do right, even while we are failing to fulfil it ; a hope of recovery which a being whose rational principle was itself corrupted (such as we picture the Devil as being) could never entertain.

But to man Kant does not deny the hope of recovery. Such recovery however must, as we have seen, take the form not of a gradual reform, but of

[1] Hor. *Sat.* i. 1. 69, 70 ; quoted H. vi. 136.

a revolution in the heart, of a *conversion* ; a change tantamount, as Kant says, quoting St. John's Gospel,[1] to a new birth or new creation. Such a conversion is not indeed speculatively explicable ; but is no less so than the fall which it reverses. Gradual reform is indeed required ; it is needed for the sensibility, as is the revolution of conversion for the mind ; but the virtue thus attained is not what should be, as too often it is, held up for admiration ; for ' however virtuous a man may be, whatever good he can do is but his duty '.[2] The one thing truly admirable in man is the original capacity for moral goodness, in which we all partake, and which is a condition *sine qua non* of our conversion. Kant hints [3] that divine co-operation *may* be necessary, whether in the way of diminishing obstacles or of affording positive assistance to our efforts ; but we are unable to know how it is supplied ; and can only endeavour to *deserve* it if any such aid be forthcoming. Nor can a man attain of himself to an assurance that his change of heart is irrevocably accomplished. The bottom of his heart must be inscrutable to himself ; but, if his disposition be fundamentally improved, he can advance in hope of arriving by his own efforts (for otherwise the attainment would have no moral value) at the goal of the way in which he has begun to tread.

Very noteworthy is the attitude here taken up by Kant towards the notion of divine Grace. He

[1] iii. 5 ; quoted and compared with Gen. i. 2, H. vi. 141.
[2] H. vi. 143.   [3] H. vi. 146.

observes [1]—in a final foot-note to this first section of his book—that he has dealt at the end of each of the four sections with a *parergon* of ' Religion within the limits of mere Reason ' ; a matter, that is to say, which does not strictly belong to it, but as it were builds upon it. These four *parerga* are (1) works of grace, (2) miracles, (3) mysteries, (4) means of grace.

The Reason, conscious of its insufficiency to accomplish the needs of our moral nature, forms a conception—or, according to Kant's distinction of the terms, an *idea*—of some supernatural operation which may supply its defects. It does not dispute the possibility or even the reality of such operations, but it cannot find in them either additions to knowledge or principles of practice. Not the former, because they cannot be presented in a possible experience under the forms of space and time ; nor the latter, because to wait for an operation of grace upon us before acting would be to forget that all moral goodness to which we can aspire must lie in action proceeding, not from others, but from ourselves. To fancy that we have an inner experience of such operations would be to open the door to what Kant calls *Schwärmerei*, or fanatical enthusiasm, a state of mind of which he always stood greatly in dread, as deadly to sober thought and conduct. Therefore we must confine ourselves, as regards divine grace, to the *effort to deserve* its assistance and the *hope* that it may assist us if we do

[1] H. vi. 146 *n*.

deserve it ; since we can neither immediately apprehend its working in ourselves, nor understand the
mode in which it operates ; and thus cannot take it
into account either theoretically or practically.

Although Kant's insistence that all right action
must be our own, and his refusal to see in alleged
experiences of grace anything but illusion, in ' waiting
for power from on high ' anything but a contradiction
of the essentially active nature of moral goodness
might seem to suggest that he must be reckoned as a
Pelagian, this would not be a satisfactory classification
of his position. His emphasis on the fact of original
sin, and the stress laid by him upon conversion as
contrasted with gradual improvement, separate his
view decisively from any which regards sin as merely
the *following* of Adam ; for him the propensity to evil
is no less deeply rooted in our nature than if we had
inherited it ; though in what is our *own* nature, not in
what, being inherited, is *not* our own, but another's,
from whom we have it. ' We have sinned in Adam ',
as he quotes[1] (apparently, as Dr. Abbott[2] points out,
following the Vulgate of Rom. v. 12 in taking ἐφ' ᾧ to
mean ' in whom ') ; the experience related of Adam
is the experience of us all.

His fear that a claim to be sensible in oneself of
the effects of grace may lead to *Schwärmerei*, and that
Schwärmerei is perilous to morality is by no means
wholly unreasonable ; indeed he probably spoke
from experience. It is an old story that ' justification
by faith ' may be perverted into ' justification by

[1] H. vi. 136.　　[2] *Kant's Theory of Ethics*, p. 350 *n.*

feeling ' when it is forgotten that the faith which justifies is a faith ' working by love '; that the ' intelligible revolution ', as Kant calls it, of conversion will be exhibited in a gradual improvement of conduct, although we cannot from a gradual improvement infer a change of maxim. The denial to us of a right to rely on supposed direct perceptions of the operation of grace upon our souls is not a denial of the reality of grace itself. Kant's view (to which we shall come later) of the imputation of holiness to the converted man, in whom there is empirically only a remote approximation thereto, is *grace*, though not a sensible operation of grace. A doctrine of sensible operations of grace may actually run counter to one in which the grace of God works in us both to *will* and to *do*, not to supplement our doing, still less to make it unnecessary. Kant neither makes *doing* a ' deadly thing ', nor does he suppose that we become perfect in time by our own efforts.

We may ask further whether the Kantian doctrine is compatible with belief in the *forgiveness of sins*. This might, at first sight, especially as it has often been described as something of which we may have assurance through feeling, seem to be just such a sensible operation of grace as Kant's rational theology will not admit. Of course the doctrine has often been criticized as immoral, and it has certainly sometimes been so preached as to encourage immorality. But forgiveness is, rightly regarded, not a work of grace for which we have to wait—Kant would have us wait for nothing of the kind—but as something already there : it precedes conversion, which is our own act indeed, but one which we cannot fathom ; we cannot understand, as it were from outside, how the bad man can become good. So far as the change is, even to the converted man himself, inscrutable, it can be represented, without detriment to morality, as due to the pardoning act of God.

We have no doubt to admit that there is in Kant a singular lack of the unction which, in some writers on religion, and even in some philosophers, kindles and feeds in their readers the flame of pious feeling. It is however part of the value of his work that it lacks an attraction, the presence of which has too often served as an apology for lack of thoroughness in thought. Moreover the dryness of the presentation in other respects throws into stronger relief the depth and earnestness of his moral sentiment, inspired by which he teaches us that there is no *getting round* God, as it were, whether by knowledge or by ceremonial ; for God is only apprehensible by us in and through our moral obedience to the law which we know by its own ' manifest authority ' to be the expression of his will. This is Kant's fundamental thought about religion and his principal contribution to the philosophy of it.

The second part of *Religion within the Limits of Mere Reason* deals with the strife of the Good Principle with the Evil for lordship over mankind.

The existence of a principle within us which resists the Good Principle is, Kant here points out,[1]

[1] H. vi. 151.

implied by the expression *Virtue*—ἀρετή, *virtus*, *Tugend*—which, implying as it does high spirit and courage, presupposes an enemy to be overcome. Virtue in this sense was the watchword of the Stoics, whose manly exhortations are considered by Kant preferable to the promptings of the lazy spirit which is content to wait upon divine assistance. Yet the Stoics erred in seeking their enemy in the undisciplined inclinations of our animal nature, instead of a more dangerous principle, lurking in ambush 'behind the Reason itself'. They therefore ascribed to man an unperverted will to adopt the moral law into his maxims ; he was merely hindered in carrying this will into effect by the strength of the natural appetites. But the real trouble is that one does not *will* to go against the natural appetites, when they prompt us to transgress the law. The appetites or inclinations, which in themselves are neither good nor evil, are opposed to *principles* in general ; hence *any* noble principle of morality has a certain disciplinary value in controlling them ; but *mere* discipline, such as the Stoics recommended, may only bring about a seeming peace, and not overcome the true enemy, namely the perverted will. Unless virtue contend against *that* enemy, all virtues are, if not, as a Father of the Church said,[1] *splendida vitia* (*glänzende Laster*), at least *glänzende Armseligkeiten*,[2] mere tinsel, as it were, the mere outside appearance of something fine, but possessed of no intrinsic moral

---

[1] The doctrine (not the phrase) is Augustine's ; see e. g. *de Civ. Dei*, xix. 25.   [2] H. vi. 152 *n*.

value. Hence, despite his admiration for Stoicism (the temper of which he obviously prefers to that of Pietism), he sees a profounder truth in the Christian representation of the Evil Principle as an evil Spirit without us—so long as we do not take this representation for information about the supersensible world, which of course his ' critical ' philosophy could not admit. For this representation completely avoids the confusion of the Evil Principle with mere natural inclination, and yet does not remove our responsibility, since we are to blame for our understanding with the Devil, and subjection to him ; while again, in making the opposite of heaven not earth (the sphere of the life of appetite), but hell, this same Christian representation of the matter emphasizes the great gulf which is fixed between the principles of moral goodness and moral evil, as between light and darkness ; which else tend to be represented as merely greater and less degrees of illumination.

The only end of God's creation conceivable, Kant proceeds to affirm [1]—conceivable, that is (of course) from a *moral* point of view—is *Man in his moral perfection.* The *idea* of Man in his moral perfection as that the realization whereof is the only conceivable end which God, as a holy being, can be supposed to have set before himself in creating the world, may thus be represented as eternally existent in him, not made by him, but essential to his being, his only-begotten Son ; as the Word by which all things else are made, and without which was not

[1] H. vi. 155.

anything made that was made. Our moral consciousness sets this idea before us as a pattern, after the imitation of which we may strive ; and that from no other motive except that supplied by the idea itself, which is thus the source of our power to strive after it. The idea presents itself to us, not as a creation of our own, but as though descended to us from heaven. For the presence of radical evil in ourselves as earthly men prevents us from conceiving the Ideal as that of an earthly man who has become good and heavenly ; we must conceive it rather as a heavenly ideal become earthly ; and this can only be set before the imagination as the life of a Man who went about doing good by teaching and example among those around him, and exhibited his own goodness—Kant always, we remember, tends to suppose that goodness can only be warranted pure when it goes against interest and inclination—in endurance of suffering, even to a bitter death, for the sake of the world's advantage and even for that of his own enemies. The only hope of pleasing God then for man will lie in that practical faith in this incarnate Son of God, whereby a man makes his own the disposition which is thus exemplified in him.

The objective reality of this idea of the Son of God lies, says Kant,[1] in our morally legislative Reason. As he so often insists, the ' ought ' of the moral law implies the ' can '. We have thus all that we need in the way of the objective reality of the Ideal whereat we are bound to aim. To demand that we be certi-

[1] H. vi. 157.

fied that this Ideal has actually been manifested in history, or to require that its authority be attested by miracles, is proof of a 'moral unbelief' which does not recognize the Ideal presented to us by reason as a sufficient motive to action. Hence actions which should be rendered possible only in consequence of such—to Kant's thinking—irrelevant confirmations of the reality of the Ideal would be morally worthless. Moreover, since experience never uncovers to any of us, even in his own case, the depths of the heart, what is really important in the example afforded by the picture of an ideally perfect life, namely that it should be an example, not merely of outward conformity to the law, but of inward holiness, could never be certified by historical or miraculous evidence addressed to experience.

While thus removing altogether from the sphere of 'Religion within the limits of mere Reason' the consideration of historical evidence, Kant hints [1] that emphasis on a miraculous or exceptional origin or nature in the Pattern Man might tend to lessen the force of his example. But all curious questions about the Son of God, apart from the appropriation of the disposition exemplified in him, he sets aside as vain and destitute of all moral value. This disposition we recognize as not being our own, so far as our lives are not faultless; we see it exemplified in Christ, as he is represented to us in the Gospels, and we have no evidence of inconsistency in his case between his life and his principles; so that he can

[1] H. vi. 158.

ask ' Which of you convinceth me of sin ? ' [1] This disposition however remains not ours but another's, except so far as it can be appropriated by us ; but the possibility of such an appropriation (which is of course what is meant by the traditional doctrine of the imputation to us of the merits of Christ) labours under certain very grave difficulties, to the consideration of which Kant now turns.[2]

The first difficulty is this : How can man *in time* fulfil the infinite requirements of the law to ' be perfect as our Father which is in heaven is perfect ' ? [3] The answer of Kant is that this concerns man only as phenomenon ; the principle in the heart is independent of time, and God, who knows the heart, can see in the principle which after a true conversion determines a man's actions the perfection which does not belong to his life at any particular moment of time.

The second difficulty [4] is as follows : How can one be assured of the permanence of the right disposition ?

One can only be thus assured, we are told, in retrospect, on comparison of the life before and the life after conversion ; and, according to the evidence thus obtained, judge of the present nature of our disposition and the promise which it gives of a future, whether good or evil. Where the disposition to which our experience thus witnesses is good and pure, it is that which is described in Scripture as the

[1] John viii. 46.   [2] H. vi. 161.   [3] Matt. v. 48.
[4] H. vi. 162.

' Comforter ', the divine Spirit bearing witness with our spirit that we are the children of God.[1]

The prospect here mentioned of goodness or badness confirmed and enduring, and the hopes and fears based thereon bring up the question of eternal punishment, to which Kant devotes a long foot-note.[2] The question whether future punishments are everlasting or no he reckons as a childish one, which should not be asked as though a dogmatic answer were possible. Such an answer, whichever it might be, would be unfortunate in its moral effects. The assertion that punishment will *not* be everlasting may excite a hope of being able to hold out—he quotes a sailor mentioned in a book of travels as expressing such a hope. On the other hand, the assertion that it *will* be everlasting leads to insincere death-bed consolation, administered by clergymen who cannot bring themselves to be cruel when asked for comfort, and so hold out hopes of a conversion when the time for it is past. Any dogmatic decision on the subject then is in Kant's judgement unjustifiable and harmful ; but the man who is conscious of no increasing security in goodness looks forward to an infinite series of bad acts, just as one who is conscious of growth in goodness looks forward to an infinite series of good acts ; because, if there be a life to come, there is nothing to warrant us in assigning a limit to either series.

The third difficulty [3] is this : How, even if a man

[1] John xiv. 26, Rom. viii. 16.   [2] H. vi. 164 ff.
[3] H. vi. 166.

should do nothing wrong after his conversion can he make satisfaction for the guilt of sins committed before conversion ? Kant's suggested solution is that God takes the change of heart at his conversion, when he becomes a new man, as the discharge of the debt that he had previously incurred. The ' new man ' is at once one with the old and another than he ; physically the same, morally another. As the new man that he now is, he accepts the punishment of his previous sins as good ; though the ' old man ' in him feels it as an evil. This new man in us is our Redeemer and Advocate. From the empirical point of view the imputation to us of this new humanity is always a matter of grace. The value of this doctrine lies in its *negative* bearing, in emphasizing the absolute necessity, for relief from the burden of past sins, of a change of heart ; for which no ingratiating of oneself with God by prayers or praises can possibly serve as a substitute.

In the second division of the second section of the treatise on *Religion within the Limits of Mere Reason* Kant discusses the claim of the Evil Principle to lordship over man and the mutual strife of the two Principles, the evil and the good, for this lordship.

Kant begins [1] by observing that the holy Scripture, in its Christian part, the New Testament, expresses the intelligible moral relation which is the subject of this part of his work, in the form of a history, wherein two Principles, as diametrically opposed to one another as hell to heaven, are represented as persons

[1] H. vi. 174.

outside of man—which not only essay their power, the one against the other, to obtain dominion over him, but also desire to make good their claims as of right before a Supreme Judge, the one as man's accuser, the other as his advocate.

According to this myth—as we may properly call a history thus intended to express an eternal truth— man was originally invested with property over all earthly goods, on condition of holding them only as of tenant right, *dominium utile,* under his Creator and Lord as proprietor (*dominus directus*). There is also an evil being—how he had become so evil as to be untrue to his lord, seeing he was originally good, is unknown—who has, by his fall, forfeited all the property which he might have had in heaven, and now wishes to acquire for himself another property on earth. To him now, as to a being of a higher grade—as a spirit—earthly and material objects could afford no satisfaction, and so he seeks to acquire a dominion over *hearts,* by making the first parents of all men revolt from their Sovereign and become dependent upon him; and so he succeeds by this means in making himself the proprietor of all the goods of the earth, that is, as he is called in Scripture,[1] ' prince of this world '.

Now one might here find it difficult to understand why God did not use his power against this traitor and destroy the kingdom which he desired to establish, rather at the outset of his attempt than afterwards. The explanation of this difficulty

[1] John xii. 31, xiv. 30, xvi. 11.

however is found in the fact that the government and control exercised by Supreme Wisdom over rational beings treats them according to the principle of their freedom, and they must be able to put to their own credit whatever good or evil they may win. Kant tells in a note [1] a story from the narrative of a French missionary to the Iroquois Indians in North America, Père Charlevoix, to the effect that when he had told a catechumen of all the evil which the Evil Spirit had introduced into the original creation of God, and of his continued endeavours to frustrate God's best designs, the Iroquois asked indignantly, ' But why does not God kill the Devil ? ' Père Charlevoix candidly admits, says Kant, that to this question he could not on the spur of the moment find any answer.

The Devil then became in this manner the prince of this world ; and set up, in despite of the Good Principle, a kingdom of evil, to which all men naturally descended from Adam should be subject, and that with their own good will, because the glitter of this world's goods diverted their attention from the depth of the ruin for which they were reserved. Yet the Good Principle kept open his claim to lordship over man by means of the establishment of a form of government, in the shape of the Jewish theocracy, ordained merely for the public exclusive honouring of his Name ; while the hearts of the subjects of this theocracy continued to be determined by no other attraction than that

[1] H. vi. 174 f.

of this world's goods, and thus could only be ruled by rewards and punishments awarded in this life.

In such a condition of affairs, no other laws were adequate than such as in part prescribed burdensome ceremonies and customs which in part indeed were ethical, but, when ethical, only of the sort that included external compulsion, and were thus merely *civil*, not affecting the inner moral sentiment or disposition. Thus this dispensation effected no essential breach in the kingdom of darkness, but only served to keep ever in mind the inalienable rights of the original proprietor. In the same people, at a time when the evils arising from a hierarchical constitution of this kind had come to be felt in full measure—and that all the more probably in consequence of the influence of the doctrine of freedom taught by the Greek philosophers—so that the people was ripe for a revolution, there appeared a Person who, while a man in his teaching and example, announced himself as a messenger from heaven, not implicated in Adam's guilt, so that the prince of this world had nothing in him. Kant here inserts a foot-note on the belief that this immunity from sin was secured by birth from a Virgin, and points out both the congruity of this idea with certain moral instincts and sundry difficulties, doctrinal and physiological, which may be raised about it ; and concludes with dismissing any controversy on the subject as idle, since the doctrine has no practical value except as a symbol of a humanity free from anything which hinders a victorious resistance to evil.

Alarmed for the safety of his kingdom, the prince of this world persecutes this perfect man, and eventually brings about his death in torment without however being able to subdue his will ; the physical victory of the Evil Principle is thus the moral victory of the Good. The descent of the Good Principle from heaven into man cannot be assigned merely to a certain date ; it must be held to have taken place invisibly from the beginnings of our race ; but the manifestation of it in a real man as an example for others can be described in the words of the Fourth Gospel—' he came unto his own, and his own received him not, but as many as received him, to them gave he power to become the sons of God, even to them that believe on his Name ' [1]—that is, as Kant expounds the text, he opens the gate of freedom to all who are willing like him to die to all that keeps them, to the detriment of their moral condition, chained to earthly life ; and gathers such into ' a people chosen for his peculiar possession, zealous in good works ',[2] leaving those still in bondage who prefer moral slavery to freedom. Thus the moral outcome of the duel between the heroes of the story down to the death of Christ is not the subjugation of the Evil Principle but the breaking of his power and the setting up of another kingdom, in which deserters from his can take refuge.

Thus Kant presents the sacred history of Chris-

[1] John i. 11, 12. [2] Tit. ii. 14.

tianity as containing under a 'mystical husk' a universally valid truth ; namely, that there is no salvation at all for men, except in their sincere adoption of true ethical principles into their disposition ; that this adoption is resisted not merely by their sensible inclinations but by the perversity common to all men ; which can only be overcome by taking as our principle of action the idea of moral goodness in its purity, with the consciousness that it really belongs to our original state, and that man has only to take pains to keep it free from impure admixture and to allow it to penetrate our disposition, in order to become convinced that the forces of evil (the gates of hell) [1] are powerless to destroy it. He must not, Kant insists, attempt to compensate for lack of this conviction superstitiously (*aberglaubisch*) by expiations, or fanatically (*schwärmerisch*) by inner illuminations, but must trust to the evidence of a good course of life.

To this section is appended 'a general remark' on the second of the four 'parerga' of national religion previously enumerated—viz. on miracles. Kant is not concerned to deny the possibility of their occurrence at the end of a dispensation which had been itself accredited by miracles, and serving the purpose of facilitating the passage of its votaries to a worship 'in spirit and in truth',[2] which must in the end be able to dispense with such assistance. But they must not, he holds, be made parts of Religion by representing the knowledge of them and

[1] Matt. xvi. 18.   [2] John iv. 23.

belief in them as contributing to make us well pleasing to God, for only the performance of one's duty can do that. Miracle he defines as an event the laws of whose causation are and must remain unknown to us. They may be ascribed to God, or to inferior spirits, usually to devils : ' the good angels (I know not why) give little or no occasion for being talked about '. He notes that common sense, even in those who believe past miracles, generally rejects new ones. Miracles can however be of no real moral value. They attest nothing ; rather they must themselves be attested as divine by their conformity to moral laws ; but the fact that Satan can transform himself into an angel of light [1] makes this an uncertain test. He dismisses as sophistical any attempts to defend the rarity of miracles as rendering them more credible than would their frequent occurrence.

The third section of Kant's great work on Religion deals with the Victory of the Good Principle over the Evil, and Foundation of a Kingdom of God upon earth.

Freedom from the law of sin having been once won, it is still, Kant declares, continually imperilled by the assaults of evil ; thus the condition even of the converted, or, as Kant says, the ' morally well-disposed ' man is always one of continual conflict. The sphere of these assaults is human society : not the ' raw individual nature ', but the social intercourse of man with man, stirs up the evil passions which work

---

[1] 2 Cor. xi. 14.

havoc in his soul. ' It is enough ', says Kant, with his characteristic tendency to pessimism in respect of social intercourse, ' that his fellows are there, that they surround him, and that they are human beings, for them mutually to corrupt one another and make one another bad.' Hence the defence against these assaults must likewise take a social form—that of the creation of a society for the maintenance of morality. The extension of such a society when once founded to embrace the whole race of mankind (and so to exclude all social influences making for evil) is propounded to us by reason as a problem and a duty, ' for thus alone can there be hopes of a victory of good over evil '. Such an ' ethical society ', if its laws be recognized as of public authority, becomes an *ethischbürgerliche Gesellchaft* as opposed to a *rechtlichbürgerliche Gesellschaft* wherein only legal and not moral obligation is recognized ; an ' ethical commonwealth ' as one may perhaps translate Kant's expression. This may exist within the political commonwealth, it may even consist of the same members (that it should be so is of course the Reformers' ideal of a national Church, as we find it e.g. in Hooker) ; nor could it arise, except the political commonwealth were there to give it a foundation whereon to build. But its principle is different from that of the political commonwealth ; it is not *law*, with its attendant compulsion, but *virtue*, in respect of which compulsion, reaching as it does only the exterior conduct, not the inner disposition, can have no place. ' Woe ', says Kant, ' to the lawgiver who proposes to give effect by compulsion to a constitution directed to ethical ends. For thereby he will not only effect just the opposite to the ethical aim, but he will also undermine the political and make it insecure.' Some may perhaps see in this remark a prescient warning against the policy of ' Prohibition ' adopted by the legislature of a great nation in our own days.

The ethical State or Kingdom of Virtue has, Kant tells us, objective reality, so far as it is actually the duty of man to unite to form it, but subjectively we can never hope that the good wills of men should so devote themselves to a united effort to promote this end as to secure its perfect realization.

The first division of this section is occupied by what Kant designates as a 'philosophical'—philosophical, that is, as opposed to historical—representation of the victory of the Good Principle by means of the foundation of a Kingdom of God upon earth ; and this itself begins with a chapter on the ' ethical state of nature '. With the *political* state is contrasted, says Kant, a state of nature, wherein every man is, in the absence of any public authority, a law to himself : and in like manner we may oppose to the ' ethical commonwealth ' a corresponding ' ethical state of nature ', wherein each man stands by himself without any judge to whom he and others alike owe submission : and even in the political commonwealth itself, where each several citizen is no longer in the juristic state of nature, but is the subject of some sovereign, each citizen nevertheless remains still as a citizen of the political commonwealth, in an ethical state of nature. For, as it is of the essence of an ethical commonwealth or kingdom of virtue to be a voluntary union, any constraint placed by the political commonwealth upon its individual citizens to join an ethical commonwealth contradicts the essence of this latter kind of society, which must admit no internal interference by the political State, although its formation is subject to the negative condition that no arrangements of the ethical commonwealth should be in contradiction with the duties of its members as citizens of the political commonwealth. This, however, Kant thinks is a condition of no practical importance where the ethical bond is genuinely such. The distinction of the ethical from the political commonwealth, of Church from State, is characterized not only by this internal independence of the former upon the latter but by what we may call (though Kant does not use the word) the Catholicity of the national Church, which never claims to be the ethical commonwealth but only a branch thereof.

It is hardly necessary to do more now than to call attention to this interesting indication of Kant's mind upon this subject of the relations of Church and State. I shall content myself with pointing out, without wishing to lay too much stress upon the point, that it betrays the influence of the traditional Lutheran attitude in regard to the matter. This is distinguished alike from that of the Roman Catholic Church and that of the Reformed or Calvinistic

Churches by its tendency to leave to the State all matters relating to the ordering of outward conduct and to consider the Church as concerned only with the individual conscience.[1]

The title of the next ensuing chapter runs as follows: ' Man must depart from the ethical State of nature to become a member of an ethical Commonwealth.'[2] Hobbes's description of the State of nature as *bellum omnium contra omnes* is, says Kant, correct, if for *bellum* we read *status belli*. (This, by the way, is perhaps not more of a correction than Hobbes's own qualification in the *Leviathan*, when he says that ' the Nature of War consisteth not in actual fighting but in the known Disposition thereto during all the Time there is no Assurance to the contrary '.[3]) Just as every man must leave this primitive state of nature to enter into the state of political union, so it is a duty to leave the ethical state of nature to become a member of an ethical commonwealth. This is a duty *sui generis*, owed not by man to man, but by mankind to itself ; but the idea of an ethical commonwealth, although ' reason requires of us that we should aim at realizing it ', is a *common* end, which it is not laid as an obligation on the individual, as such, to realize. It is thus an Idea of Reason, bringing along with it the idea of a higher moral Being, whose general providence may

---

[1] I may refer here to the very thorough and profound discussion of the subject in Troeltsch's *Soziallehren*. Cp. Ritschl, *Rechtfertigung und Versöhnung*, § 49 (Eng. tr., pp. 327 foll.).

[2] H. vi. 194.   [3] *Lev.* I, c. 13.

enable the separately inadequate efforts of individuals to attain the end which they have in common.

A third chapter is headed : ' The conception of an ethical Commonwealth is the conception of a People of God under ethical laws.' [1] The common lawgiver in the ethical commonwealth cannot be considered, as in the political commonwealth, to be the society itself. For we cannot think of ethical laws as originating from a superior, so as not to be binding until published by his authority. We must thus conceive of the lawgiver in an ethical common-wealth as a Being such that the laws of morality, which are those of the autonomous will—that is to say, are perceived by each man's conscience to be binding upon him in their own right—can at the same time be regarded as *his* commandments ; and as a Searcher of hearts, whose judgement upon his subjects relates not (as would those of the society) merely to their outward conduct, but to their inner motive.

Kant appends to this chapter a note on the notion of statutory divine commands distinct from those of the State.[2] Such Kant will not admit to be possible. Although the laws of the State are not in themselves divine commands, respect for them *is* divinely commanded. No laws of this kind are *more* divine ; and the Scriptural saying ' We ought to obey God rather than men ' [3] means only that, if men command what is evil in itself—contrary, that is, to the moral law—we ought not to obey them ; it is not to be taken (he means) as directing a preference

[1] H. vi. 195.   [2] H. vi. 196.   [3] Acts v. 29.

of ecclesiastical ordinances to the commands of the State.

The next chapter affirms that the idea of a People of God is under human arrangements only realizable in the form of a *Church*.[1]

The *invisible* Church, Kant tells us, is not an object of possible experience but an ideal archetype. The *visible* Church involves a distinction between pastors and flock, clergy and laity. The notes of a true Church Kant arranges according to the four classes of categories which he recognizes in the *Critique of Pure Reason* and elsewhere. 1. In *quantity* it must be *universal*, that is, one throughout the world. 2. In *quality*, *pure*, held together, that is, by none but moral motives, not by superstition or fanaticism. 3. In *relation*, *free*, both in respect of the mutual relations of its members, and in respect of the relationship between Church and State. There must be neither a hierarchy on the one hand, nor on the other hand a democratic (or rather individualistic) illuminism, where every one is severally inspired. 4. In *modality*, *unchangeable* in regard of the fundamental constitution, because founded on *a priori* foundations, namely, on the Idea of its end. Moreover it must not be monarchical (under a Pope), aristocratic (under bishops), or democratic (consisting of sectarian *illuminati*); but like the family of an invisible Father, represented by a Son who knows his will and reveals it to others.

The heading of the fifth chapter is : ' The con-

[1] H. vi. 198.

stitution of every particular Church is always based upon faith in a history, that is, in revelation, which one may call the Church faith ; and this will be best based on a sacred Scripture.' [1]

A truly universal Church, says Kant, can be based only upon a pure religious faith ; he means one based upon mere reason, and so accessible to every thinking man, as distinguished from an historical faith. For the spread of an historical faith is always conditioned by the spread of information respecting the historical facts which are its object, and by the capacity of the recipients of this information to judge of its credibility.

There is a natural tendency in human nature not to remain content with the moral, which is the only true, service of God ; and so to add to it, or even to substitute for it, a so-called ' divine service ', addressed, not, as is our *moral* service, to our fellow men, but directly to God, who is thought of as, like a human potentate, pleased by demonstrations of honour and respect. Such direct approach to and influence upon God is however not in reality possible.

How then does God desire to be served ? Is his will to be ascertained from *statutory* or from *moral* laws ? The former kind are not accessible to Reason by itself ; and even if there were such, and it became our duty to obey them as revelations of the divine will, yet this would presuppose the prior and superior obligation of the moral law, from the conception of which indeed the very conception of God itself

[1] H. vi. 200.

springs, and which allows us to contemplate but one God, and therefore only one, that is, the purely moral religion. Thus the true worshippers of God are not they who say ' Lord, Lord ', but those who do the will of God.[1]

If however we ask for our rule, not merely as men, but as members of a Church (a commonwealth, that is, established to counteract the evil effects of mutual communication among men who share the radical propensity to evil ingrained in human nature), then a statutory or revealed 'Church-faith' seems to be required. As to the form which this should take, to regard it as permanently fixed would be presumptuous and would tend to excuse us the labour of improving it ; yet a particular form may be of divine institution, when we recognize it to be completely in harmony with natural religion, and take note of its sudden appearance without, as it would seem, any adequate intellectual preparation in the public mind.

There is an unfortunate tendency in human nature to think statutory observances more pleasing to God than moral, just because the former are done solely with a view to his service. Thus, historically, an historical creed precedes a moral, temples churches, and priests clergymen (*Geistlicher* or teachers of religion) ; while the order of moral value is the reverse of this. The superiority of a Scripture to a tradition as the standard of teaching in a Church lies in its relatively greater permanence and security.

[1] Matt. vii. 21.

The whole of this chapter is of course tinged with Kant's characteristic individualism, and his conception of history as quite external, so to say, to the true significance of the values which appear in the course of it. He appends a note of some interest, in which he remarks that there can only be one Religion, properly so called, though there may be many creeds (*Glauben*). The claim however is made by separate Churches to be the only and universal Church ; and this leads to the branding of dissentients, according to the degree of their dissent, as heterodox, heretical, or infidel. Such orthodoxy, with its tendency to persecute those who vary from its formulas, may be despotic and brutal, or it may be liberal ; the former kind, he remarks, is not always found among Catholics, nor always absent among Protestants.

The sixth chapter of this section has as its title the following : ' The Church-faith has the pure faith of Religion as its supreme interpreter.' [1]

Here Kant notices an ingrained tendency in men to seek empirical confirmation for purely rational conceptions. Hence some Church-creed must be taken and interpreted—even if in a strained unnatural way—so as to convey purely moral teaching. The imprecatory Psalms for instance must not be used to justify vindictiveness ; for biblical authority is not the standard of morality but vice versa ; they may, however, be interpreted of one's enemies in the sense of wicked persons, or given a sense as relative

---

[1] H. vi. 207.

T

merely to the peculiar situation of the Jews as citizens of a theocratic State.

This kind of interpretation has always been used when a sacred Scripture was in question ; in pagan antiquity, in Judaism, in Mohammedanism, in the religion of the Vedas, as well as in Christianity ; and it is justifiable, since the only end of Scripture study is to make us better men, and the belief in historical fact is in itself dead and religiously worthless. We must then interpret Scripture by the principles of natural religion ; and this exposition of Scripture by natural religion is what we are to understand by the Spirit of God which guides us into all truth.[1]

The use of a sacred Scripture carries with it the necessity of biblical learning and exegetical science. The free pursuit of biblical and theological criticism is not to be restrained by the State, for, says Kant acutely, if it is, ' the laity would compel the clergy to conform to their own views, views which they themselves have only learned from the teaching of the clergy '.[2] The more recent history of his own Prussian Church has afforded an illustration of the truth of this observation. He goes on to insist that the objective interpretation provided by Reason, that is, by natural Religion and by biblical learning, must not be replaced by that of subjective *feeling*, which opens the way to every kind of fanaticism. Here, as elsewhere, Kant shows, probably by reaction from the extravagances of contemporary Pietism, less

[1] John xvi. 13.   [2] H. vi. 211.

sympathy with, or perhaps one should rather say
a greater dread of the intuitive or, as Baron von
Hügel calls it, the mystical element in religion than
even of the institutional, to which he allows a subordinate and provisional place by the side of the
rational or intellectual.

ch.7 A seventh chapter deals with ' the gradual
transition from the Church-faith to the sole supremacy of pure religious faith ' as constituting ' the
approach of the kingdom of God '.[1]

The Church, he says, as based on an historical faith,
as to which disputes are inevitable, may be called
militant ; but the Church, as being what it aims at
being, based upon pure religious faith, and so
universal, may be called *triumphant*. The faith
which leads to pure moral or practical service is
saving ; the faith which leads to statutory service
mercenary (the religion of the bondman). *Saving*
faith has two parts—one of which respects what
is not in our own power—namely redemption and
atonement ; the other what is in our own power—
namely a good course of life. These are inseparably
conjoined, but we can only represent what is in itself
necessary conjunction under the form of succession ;
either by saying that faith in our acquittal and absolution begets a moral life ; or that a moral life begets
faith in our acquittal or absolution. Hence there
arises an *antinomy*. On the one hand we ask : Can
any sensible man, conscious of sin in himself, suppose
that merely believing in a satisfaction made for him

[1] H. vi. 212.

will make him live a good life for the future ? He can only bring himself to do so either by supposing the precedent faith to be instilled into him from above ; or by supposing his participation in the benefits of the Atonement to be conditioned—conditioned, that is, by his own good conduct. On the other hand, how can man, with his perverted nature, hope to make himself a new creature, unless the divine justice be already appeased by the Atonement ? But this makes a belief in the Atonement a requisite antecedent to good works.

As the grounds of our Freedom are in any case inscrutable, inquiry into these alternatives will not be of any assistance to us ; but practically, if we ask whether we are to begin with faith in what God has done *for* us, or with an attempt to make ourselves worthy of whatever he may be pleased to do for us, we must surely take the latter of the two.

From the one point of view, belief in a vicarious satisfaction is our duty, while the good life is a matter of grace. From the other, the good life is our duty, the atonement is a matter of grace. Those who adopt the former position are blamed as superstitious and indifferent to morality ; those who adopt the latter as infidel or rationalistic, and as indifferent or hostile to revelation.

The solution of the antinomy which Kant proposes is that our difficulty will vanish if for an historical belief in Christ and the atonement wrought by him we substitute a rational belief in the Son of God as the archetype of a humanity well pleasing to God ;

for this kind of belief in the Son of God is not distinguishable from a life directed to the attainment of that ideal. The evolution of historical into moral religion is to be expected, so far as men can further it, not from a revolution, but from a gradual process of reformation. But the Kingdom of God may in a true sense be said to have come when the principle that the religion of reason is the goal of the Church-creed has taken root in the public mind.

So ends the first division of the third section of Kant's work. The second is occupied by an ' historical representation of the gradual foundation of the dominion of the Good Principle upon earth '.[1] This representation will probably strike any reader of our generation as extremely unhistorical. The history of Christendom is presented as little or nothing but an illustration of the Lucretian saying, *Tantum religio potuit suadere malorum* ;[2] and Kant's own age is declared to be the best of any, because Christians enjoy now a greater freedom than ever before to sit loose to the historical faith of the Church.

The history of religion in general is, for Kant, no more than a record of the conflict of the religion of outward worship with the religion of morality ; and it can only be made coherent by limiting one's view to that part of the world wherein the question between the two has been really raised and debated ; neither the religions which have no organic connexion with Christianity, nor even the Jewish religion, whose connexion with the Christian Church is only physical

[1] H. vi. 223.   [2] Lucr. i. 101.

or historical, enters into the history of the latter properly so called. For it consists—despite the excellence of the Decalogue as a summary of moral duties—of outward ordinances only ; it limits its view to this life ; and as the Jews must have had, like all other nations, the notion of another life, this limitation must have been intentional.[1]

Even monotheism is a less important distinction of Judaism than is often supposed. For the 'many gods' of paganism were subordinate to one chief ; and many gods who all agreed in requiring morality of their votaries would be better than a single god who required chiefly a statutory service. We may compare here an observation, of which Kant was almost certainly ignorant, made by St. Thomas Aquinas[2] from the other side, so to say, in which he points out that it is not the Greek paganism, with its many subordinate deities under one chief, which is essentially inconsistent with Christian monotheism, but rather the Manichean dualism, which has *two* gods of opposite *character* from a moral point of view.

Christianity then, according to Kant, should not be regarded as the offspring of Judaism. It will of course follow from this that the view now so often urged by English theologians, that the Christian Church is organically one ' People of God ' with the

---

[1] This was of course the contention of Warburton in his celebrated work on the *Divine Legation of Moses* ; and the same point is made by Archdeacon Charles in his remarkable Jowett Lectures on *Eschatology : Hebrew, Jewish, and Christian.*

[2] *Summa c. Gentiles,* i. 42 ad fin.

Church of the Old Testament, is explicitly rejected by him ; and it is interesting to observe that his estimate of Judaism as intrinsically different from Christianity was unaffected by his undoubted friendship and respect for the Jewish philosopher Moses Mendelssohn. Later on indeed we find him alluding to Mendelssohn's defence of his own loyalty to Judaism on the ground that it was admittedly the foundation of Christianity. But he takes the true meaning of the Jewish scholar to be that Christians must purge Christianity of the Judaism which remains in it, before they can reasonably expect the Jews to consider a summons to exchange their own religion for it.

An unsympathetic account of the history of the Christian Church in the primitive and medieval periods follows, which ends in Kant repeating the exclamation of the Roman poet which I have already quoted, ' *Tantum religio potuit suadere malorum !* ' [1] He remarks that all through there shines in the pages of the Gospels the purely moral interest of the Founder of Christianity himself. The present age of the Church is, however, undoubtedly the best, for the reason mentioned above.

Kant proceeds to offer a moral commentary on the apocalyptic representations of the future triumph of the true religion ; and sees in St. Paul's prophecy [2] that ' when all things shall be subdued unto him, then shall the Son also himself be subject unto him that put all things under him, that God may be all in

[1] H. vi. 230.   [2] 1 Cor. xv. 28.

all ' a forecast of a time when there shall fall away from the pure religion of reason that husk of historical or ecclesiastical faith with which it is as yet unable to dispense.

According to a well-known story, Frederick the Great once asked one of his chaplains for a compendious argument in favour of Christianity, and was answered in the brief phrase 'The Jews, your Majesty '. Without mention of this story (which may well have been in his mind) Kant inserts [1] a note in the course of which he dismisses this ' edifying ' explanation of the persistence of the older creed in spite of the dispersion of its adherents. It is to be explained merely by the fact of their possession of a sacred book, as is the similar persistence of the Zoroastrianism of the Parsees, despite their expulsion from Persia.

The third section has like the two preceding its Scholion or appendix on a *parergon* of Religion.[2] As the third *parergon* we have *Mysteries* (*Geheimnisse*). There are *arcana* of Nature, *secreta* of statecraft, which may be so called ; but we are here concerned with *sacred* mysteries, *heilige Geheimnisse*. These are not mysteries which we do not know but might learn ; nor is anything rightly called a mystery which lies open to all, like the Freedom of the Will, though the ground thereof is inscrutable and a mystery. But the idea of the Supreme Good, an idea itself bound up with the pure moral sentiment, does give rise— since a man cannot by himself, or by the help of other

[1] H. vi. 235.   [2] H. vi. 236.

men, realize this idea—to the idea of a divine co-operation. This *is* a mystery. For we do not know what or how much is to be ascribed to such co-operation. We only know what we have to do to render ourselves worthy of it. But the so-called 'mystery' of the Trinity is not rightly so described, since it only regards God, not in his own nature, but in reference to moral agents. It may however be, so far as first taught in Christianity, regarded as the revelation of what (through mankind's own fault) was previously a mystery, namely that God's will and nature are only to be learned from the witness of the moral law. Unconsciously repeating a favourite reflection of Abelard,[1] Kant observes that whenever suggested it appeals at once to reason ; and so we find something of the sort in many faiths, in Zoroastrianism, Hinduism, and the ancient Egyptian and Gothic religions ; perhaps even in Judaism, as the Pharisees in the Fourth Gospel do not object to the assertion that God has a Son, but only to Jesus claiming to be that Son.[2] The Trinity, as described by Kant, is of course what theologians have called an 'economic' Trinity ; but the principles of the Critical Philosophy made any doctrine of an essential Trinity out of the question for him ; so that the limitation of his affirmation to

[1] An author by whose philosophy of religion we are, as I have pointed out in the chapter devoted to him in my *Studies in the History of Natural Theology*, not infrequently reminded of Kant's. See especially pp. 218, 231.

[2] John v. 18.

3083 U

0

an ' economic ' Trinity does not imply the affirmation of an undifferentiated unity in the background. The point at issue between the orthodox and the Sabellians was in fact not really the point with which Kant is concerned in saying that the doctrine of the Trinity is not an account of the divine nature in itself. The Church is not interested in holding the doctrine in question to relate to *God in himself* as distinguished from *God going out of himself* or manifesting himself. On the contrary, it is essentially a doctrine of such a manifestation, of an eternal ' generation ' and ' procession '. It is interested, no doubt, in holding that the Trinitarian distinction is not something which we can get *behind* ; but this Kant does not assert, nor does he think it possible.

The Trinity which he acknowledges is the Trinity of the holy Lawgiver, gracious Ruler, and righteous Judge.[1] As will be seen at once, this corresponds to the familiar triad of powers in the State, the legislative, executive, and judicial ; these need not in an ethical community be, as in a political they should be, lodged in different hands ; but the recognition of the moral qualities which correspond to them as personally distinct from each other within the unity of the Godhead prevents an anthropomorphism which, by envisaging them as exercised by a single person, would assimilate God to a despotic sovereign, and suggest that the same kind of service as a despotic sovereign asks of his subjects would be acceptable to him.

[1] H. vi. 238.

This doctrine of the Trinity does not extend our knowledge of God's nature in itself, and, if presented as if it did, it would be a morally useless mystery of the kind which a rational religion cannot admit ; but, understood of God's moral relation to us, it is, in another and better sense of the word, a ' mystery ', or rather three mysteries, *revealed* to us through our own reason, and so *practically* clear to us, although presenting problems which are *theoretically* insoluble.

We believe that God is *holy*—neither indulgent nor arbitrary ; is *gracious* or *benign*—but only as pleased with our good conduct ; and is *righteous*, so as neither on the one hand to be turned from the path of justice by prayer, nor on the other to exact an impossible conformity with the holiness of the lawgiver himself,—but as limiting benignity by the condition of our conformity to the holy law, so far as human nature will admit.

The first of the three mysteries is that of *Vocation*. This implies the freedom of a creature ; and the creation of free beings is unintelligible to our *theoretical* reason ; but, notwithstanding, from the *moral* point of view the meaning of vocation is perfectly clear to us.

The second mystery is that of *Satisfaction*. We cannot *understand* how we can satisfy the demands of the law, how any one else can satisfy them for us ; but there is a *moral* necessity to assume the reality of a satisfaction, although we cannot penetrate the mystery of it by any process of reasoning. We do our best ; and God takes this imperfect performance as adequate.

The third mystery is the mystery of *Election*. Given the Satisfaction, the practical faith which appropriates it is required, yet man's perverted nature cannot produce this ; and so, when it is present, it is attributed to grace. But then why do some enjoy this grace, some not ? We cannot attribute this to the righteousness of those who are chosen, but to an inscrutable Wisdom—whose rule is to us a *mystery*.

Like the mystery of the production of organic beings, these religious mysteries we can indeed *understand*, knowing that the thing is so, and involves no contradiction ; but how it comes to pass we cannot *conceive*.

Before leaving Kant's version of the doctrine of the Trinity, we may note that he regards the Holy Spirit, not the Son, as properly the judicial power in the Godhead. The Son judges in love or goodness, and distinguishes the relatively worthy or unworthy ; the Spirit judges in righteousness, and decides who is guilty or not guilty. Thus Kant reconciles the article of the creed which ascribes judgement to the Son with three passages of the Fourth Gospel ; the first of which says that God ' sent not his Son to judge the world ' ; the second that ' he who believes not in the Son is judged already ', namely by that Spirit of whom it is said in the third that ' he shall judge the world because of sin and because of

[1] John iii. 17, John iii. 18, and John xvi. 8.

righteousness ' ; for so Kant quotes John xvi. 8, though here Luther has not ' *richten* ' but ' *strafen* ', the Greek being not κρινεῖ but ἐλέγξει.

Before passing on to the fourth and last section of the book before us, I will add a few words of comment on the doctrines we have just been discussing.

The two main points which Kant makes are (1) the inadequacy of the empirical life in time to the fulfilment of the requirements of the moral law ; and (2) the essential immorality of any religion which seeks in any way to *get round* the moral law, as it were, and obtain God's favour by any other method than obedience to its commands.

In connexion with (1) we have to consider (*a*) his characteristic *dualism* ; the sharp line which he draws here between the empirical and the noumenal self : and (*b*) his *unhistorical* attitude, for which the actual development of reality in time falls outside, so to say, of the eternal world of values (the phrase is not his), which at the best it only exhibits or symbolizes. In the historic process itself there is for him no philosophical significance. It is just here that the idealistic movement in German philosophy of the generation after him, which culminated in Hegel, sought to correct him. Thus Hegel affirms against his dualism that the real is the rational and the rational the real,[1] that what ought to be does not fail actually to *be* ;[2] and again, that the Idea of the Absolute can only be grasped as the result of the

---

[1] *Werke*, viii. 17 (*Phil. des Rechts*, Vorrede).
[2] Ibid., vi. 406, 7 (*Log.* § 234).

process in which it has unfolded its nature, through which that is fully *explicit* which was only *implicit* in the earlier stages of its development.[1]

The fourth section of Kant's book is concerned with ' Service and False Service ' of God, that is ' under the Dominion of the Good Principle ', or (an alternative title) ' Religion and Sacerdotalism ' (*Pfaffenthum*—a word with a connotation of hostility and contempt which need not belong to that by which I have rendered it).[2]

To found a kingdom of God must be something beyond the powers of man ; God must be the founder of his own kingdom. His direct part in its foundation however is to us inscrutable : but we find within ourselves a moral obligation to do *our* part towards it by fitting ourselves to be citizens of this kingdom ; and to this end we are bound to create the organization of a commonwealth of whose constitution God is the ultimate author. As a public institution, this will require an administration (a clergy) and a people (a laity). The invisible Church and the true rational religion can know nothing indeed of an official ministry or of any ' divine service ' distinct from the discharge of our moral duties ; and as this forms the ideal goal of the visible Church, the true ' divine service ' in the latter will be that which is directed towards bringing about its own ultimate disappearance, along with all that is merely historical and statutory, by absorption into the pure rational religion of the invisible Church ;

[1] *Werke*, vi. 409, 10 (*Log.* § 237).   [2] H. vi. 249.

the ' false service ' or ' worship ' will be that which puts the means in the place of the end, the historical and statutory in the place of the rational and moral.

He passes on to discuss the Religious Service of God in general ; and begins by defining Religion (not for the first time, as we have seen) as, subjectively considered, the recognition of all our duties as divine commands. This definition (1) avoids requiring any speculative assertion, even that of the existence of God, and (2) avoids also the suggestion of special duties (*Hofdienste*, ' court services ', Kant calls them) due to God over and above our mutual duties to our fellow men ; a suggestion which has often been the cover under which priestly ambition has sheltered itself. Kant sees then in religion neither an enlargement of our speculative knowledge, nor yet a collection of special duties towards God distinct from those to our neighbour, but a peculiar way of regarding the latter. He proceeds [1] to define various terms by which it is customary to describe various points of view from which we may regard the relation between a rational or philosophical religion and one which is merely historical and statutory. We call one who makes natural religion alone morally indispensable a *Rationalist* ; one who adds to this the denial that there has been any supernatural revelation a *Naturalist* ; one who, while admitting the possibility of a revelation, denies that acquaintance with such a revelation or acceptance of it is a necessary part of religion, a *Pure Rationalist* ;

[1] H. vi. 253.

lastly, one who holds that such acceptance *is* a necessary part of it, a *Pure Supernaturalist*. There is nothing to be objected to in a revelation which (like the Christian) contains nothing that men *could* not and *should* not have discovered without the assistance of revelation, though they might not have discovered it so soon or so generally. If the circumstances of its promulgation were to be in course of time forgotten it would not affect the evidence of such a religion, which would be *objectively* natural, *subjectively* revealed ; that is, its followers would have, as a matter of their own mental history, learned from an historical authority what they ought to have been able to learn by the light of nature.

The Christian Religion may be considered either as a *natural* or as a *learned* religion. Natural religion consists in the first place of morality which points to the freedom of the will as its *causa essendi* (this is Kant's famous doctrine, in the *Critique of Practical Reason*,[1] that Freedom is the *causa essendi* of the Moral Law, and the Moral Law the *causa cognoscendi* of Freedom) ; in the second, of ideas of (*a*) God and (*b*) immortality. A Church designed to spread this religion must be founded, and must impose certain statutory requirements, not indeed as *in themselves* holy acts and parts of religion, but as means of binding together the members of the society and insuring continuity of its corporate life. Kant then gives in detail the evidence from the reported discourses of Jesus for his having taught, not

[1] H. v. 4 *n*.

statutory duties, but—in contrast with the dominant Jewish view in his time—pure morality. He is particularly concerned to show that the rewards promised by Christ for good conduct are not really made the motive for it. The ' straight gate ' in the Sermon on the Mount[1] is interpreted of the good life ; the ' wide gate ' of the Church.

The Christian religion may be also considered as a *learned* religion.[2] With respect to this subject Kant takes up the position that the sacred *record* should be used to arouse attention to what is in itself plain to every man's rational apprehension. The faith thus created will be a *fides elicita*, not a *fides imperata*, or, as we may even say, *servilis*, such as is that which is found when historical belief is regarded as in the first place a duty, and learning only comes in to deal with enemies who skirmish in the rear. Biblical critics must be in the van ; the laity must follow them, including even the civil rulers. (This is probably an oblique reference to the obscurantist edict of Frederick William II. In our own time the Emperor William II followed his predecessor's example in throwing the weight of his authority into the scale of lay conservatism against the modernism of scholars like Delitzsch and Harnack.)

The second part of the fourth and last section is concerned with the False Worship (*Afterdienst*) of God in a statutory Religion ; and the first chapter of this with ' the general subjective ground of illusion in Religion '.[3] Anthropomorphism, Kant says, is

---

[1] Matt. vii. 13, 14.   [2] H. vi. 261.   [3] H. vi. 267 foll.

inevitable and harmless, so long as it does not interfere with practical religion, that is the recognition
as divine commands of our moral duties and of those
only.   Any symbol, or even (were such a thing
possible) any outward manifestation of Deity, must
be tested by the rational Ideal of moral perfection ;
to do otherwise is precisely what constitutes the
essence of *idolatry*. Of this we are guilty if we attach
a special value to religious devotion as an exhibition
of the good will ; for here we put the means—
since in Kant's view public worship (he admits no
other) is just a machinery for stimulating the moral
sentiments in us—in place of the true end, the good
disposition itself.

The following chapter deals with ' the Moral
Principle of Religion opposed to the Religious
Illusion '.[1] All that a man supposes *he* himself can
do, Kant declares, outside of a good course of life,
in order to become well-pleasing to God is mere
religious illusion and false service of God.   It is not
denied that *God* may do something, in a manner
inscrutable to us, to make us well-pleasing to him ;
but any such assistance is in the divine secrets, and
to require belief in such assistance as necessary would
be to extort by fear an act injurious to the conscience
—the confession of something of the truth whereof
we are not convinced.

He who does what he can, and trusts God to do
whatever *else* may be lacking, has a truer faith than
he who insists upon knowing what God will do, and

[1] H. vi. 270.

cherishes the hope that his *praise* of this may somehow do instead of his own moral service, whether by working a supernatural change in himself, or by procuring the favour of God. There are no limits to the extravagances of the self-sacrifice which men will attempt to substitute for a morally good life as a means of pleasing God ; nor is there any essential difference among the various surrogates for a good life offered by various religions, from pilgrimages to prayer-wheels, from statutory creeds to statutory ceremonies. Grace and Nature are wrongly opposed, for we cannot without *Schwärmerei* tell where one begins and the other ends. Fanatical (*schwärmerische*) religion is more deadly than superstition, as throwing over reason altogether, whereas superstition, though mistaking means for ends, does not do this.

We may here perhaps conveniently introduce some observations on the relation in Kant's view of *public* to *private* worship. For the latter he leaves indeed no place at all. While a ' spirit of prayer ' should (as we shall see) pervade the whole of life, the performance of special acts of prayer is to be deprecated. Such acts seem to presuppose an *imaginary* presence of God special to the worshipper, and thereby to minister to self-delusion and ' fanaticism '. They also suggest that there are duties to God other than those the obligation of which, though directly owed to others or to ourselves, we conveniently represent to ourselves as owed to a Being whose will is identified with the moral Law. A private relation to God, such as *private* prayer seems to imply, is in Kant's eyes incompatible with sound morality and sane reason. Hence he held, as I pointed out before,[1] that every man would rightly be ashamed if found on his knees alone; and it is related of him that, if a guest at his table remained standing to say his grace, he would tell him to sit down. On the other hand, little as he himself affected *public* worship, he could see a justification for it as a witness to others of our own religious disposition and an encouragement of a like disposition in them; for an inner attitude of mind could only be *communicated* through outward signs. We may here note Kant's characteristic indifference to facts to which the evolutionary psychology of a later generation has made us more attentive. The gestures and formulas of private prayer are not unnecessary, because they might be so, if there were not in our souls what we nowadays call unconscious and subconscious strata, upon which they directly act; and the dramatic element which Kant allows to exist in public worship is not wholly out of place when we are alone; for the dramatic instinct belongs to a part of our nature far more primitive and deeply rooted than that which is capable of exercising reflective thought.[2]

---

[1] *Supra*, p. 23.

[2] It is curious to find a doubtless entirely independent parallel to Kant's difficulty in seeing any justification for special acts of private prayer in a very unexpected quarter. See Richard Hurrell Froude's *Remains*, vol. i, pp. 129 foll.: 'The questions, *Why is Private Prayer a duty?* and *Why has God made it a duty?* must occur to many persons almost as often as they pray. There is something in the act itself which appears stranger and stranger to me the older I grow; and the points in which it seems so

A third chapter is devoted to ' *Pfaffenthum*
established as an established order in the False

strange are almost exclusively appropriated to it ; not bearing
at all, or any rate with much less force, on the ceremonies of
Public Worship. . . . If [a man] asks himself what is this that I find
myself engaged in ; why is it that I utter these words, and place
myself in this posture ? . . . If a man asks himself this when at
Church, a ready answer suggests itself. " The words are an
expression of just sentiments, which, though they are not yet,
ought to be, and I hope will be, mine ; and by expressing them
in this public way, I contribute to strengthen in the mind of each
person here that impression which I also experience in uniting
myself to them. Our common service too is an act of reverence
to the Master we acknowledge, in the eyes of all who deny His
authority. As to the posture, and all the ceremonial part, it is
the natural way in which I should be affected, if I perceived the
presence of Him I worship ; and therefore, a natural way of
expressing to others the tone of mind which I think suitable to
the occasion, as well as a proper respect to the feelings of those
who may perceive, in a more lively manner than myself, the
awful presence of Him I address. . . . " [The forms of Private
Prayer] must either be referred solely to the object of creating
an impression on our minds (which indeed would be absurd
enough), or at least of tending to divert contrary impressions . . .
unless we are prepared to believe that, by the act of praying, we
do something analogous to calling towards ourselves the attention
of the Deity—that we are addressing Him in a different sense
from that in which our serious thoughts can be called addresses
to Him, and that He is regarding us in a sense different from
that in which He can be said to be always regarding all things.
If, indeed, the act of praying does, in this sort, alter our relation
to the Supreme Being—if, indeed, He turns to us when we call
upon Him, then is prayer all that is said of it by those who
enforce it as a duty and extol it as a privilege ; but if anything
short of this is true, the whole is a mummery.' See article on
' The Dramatic Element in Worship ' in *The Modern Church-*
man for Dec. 1925.

Service of the Good Principle '.[1] It is hard to translate *Pfaffenthum*. I called it *Sacerdotalism* above, but it has a certain vernacular force about it which *Sacerdotalism* lacks : *Popery* is etymologically nearer, but *Pfaffenthum* does not refer so specifically to Roman Catholicism. Kant himself observes that it connotes a spiritual despotism. All false worship, he says, however outwardly superior it may seem to the religion of savages, is nevertheless essentially fetishism ; there is no difference in principle among religions except between that which makes morality the one thing needful and that which adds statutory requirements or substitutes them for it. *Godliness* should be commended to the young only as a means to *virtue* : otherwise their whole conception of God is spoiled, and an idol is presented in the place of the true God. Kant criticizes Judaism as misanthropic, Mahommedanism as proud, Hinduism as pusillanimous, and the spurious Christianity of Pietism, hoping to acquire merit by self-contempt, as servile. The chapter contains some characteristic and striking observations on the *magical* character of any form of religion which presupposes a determination of moral effects by physical causes. The relevance of these remarks to the theory of sacramental ordinances is obvious, but I reserve comment upon their bearing thereon till I come to Kant's discussion in the note on Means of Grace, appended to the concluding section of the book which we are now summarizing.

[1] H. vi. 275.

The last chapter of this section is entitled ' Of the Clue to be followed by Conscience in matters of Faith '.[1] Conscience, says Kant, cannot be guided but must be its own guide. Nothing must be risked that may be wrong : *Quod dubitas, ne feceris.* The doctrine of Probabilism that it is sufficient to justify an act that we think it *may* be right is opposed to this maxim, and is thereby rejected by Kant. He illustrates his position by the instance of religious persecution ; for that Scripture texts, e.g. ' Compel them to come in ',[2] which may seem to permit it, either have the meaning thus ascribed to them, or, if they have, are in truth a revelation of the divine will, we can never be so certain as we are of the principle that it is wrong to put to death for his religion a man otherwise innocent of any crime. He declares against the view expressed in the saying that it is better to believe too much than too little. This is an encouragement to unconscientiousness and hypocrisy. The true maxim of security is not this ; it is only that, where we are not certain of the truth or falsity of some statement alleged to be revealed which does not contradict morality, we should neither profess our faith in it, nor reject it as certainly false. The existing method of religious education, which insists on memorizing statements not certainly true, is only calculated to generate hypocrites. This chapter is to be very carefully considered, for there can be no question that there is a real danger of destroying sensitiveness of conscience in oneself or

[1] H. vi. 285.   [2] Luke xiv. 23.

others in respect of intellectual sincerity and veracity involved in acquiescence in the affirmation and inculcation of formulas of whose truth we are doubtful, and in the performance and encouragement of practices presupposing beliefs which we do not confidently entertain. On the other hand it cannot be denied that Kant, in his abstract individualism, does not seem to feel the practical problem presented by the fact that men are never isolated individuals but members of societies with historical traditions, the influence of which cannot be escaped by merely refusing to conform to certain customs, nor are all of them at the same level of intellectual and moral development. If one compares Kant in the passage we are now considering with Pascal in the *Pensées*[1] advising us to put our money on the Christian religion as the safer investment, and to induce faith by acting as if one believed, taking holy water, having masses said, and the like, and asks oneself whether the German or the Frenchman gives the nobler counsel, I, for one, should not hesitate to say 'the former'. But Kant is not sufficiently alive to the existence in us of what Pascal calls *l'automate*,[2] the 'unconscious' as we call it nowadays, nor to the truth which Butler expresses in his famous saying that 'Probability is the very guide of life'.[3] A course which neither attempts to save one's own soul by cutting (where we can, which is not by any means everywhere) the ligaments which connect

---

[1] Ed. Faugère, ii. 166.   [2] Ibid., p. 174.
[3] *Analogy*, Introd.

us with the physical and social orders in which our
individual lives are rooted, nor yet abandons us to
drift along the stream of traditional and habitual
piety, but accepts as the condition of that warfare
which our life on earth, even our religious life, must
ever be, the sense of a perpetual tension between
the individual reason and conscience and the inherited results of a past development which has
rendered the action of these possible—such a course,
as it is on the whole the more difficult, is also the one
perhaps approved in the last resort as the best by
our reason and conscience themselves, which constitute our ultimate tribunal.

I pass to the General Remark which concludes
this section and the whole work, and which is concerned with Means of Grace (*Gnadenmittel*).[1] The
only true ' means of grace ' in Kant's view is a
morally good life ; this, and this alone, will make us
deserve any such supernatural assistance as may be
necessary to supplement our best endeavours, and
so (if such assistance be forthcoming) will be the only
means towards obtaining it which we ought to adopt.

Other so-called ' means of grace ' are only, as such,
invented to evade the necessity of adopting the one
true means, a good life. They may however have
a use as outward symbols of the true service of God,
which, wholly consisting as it does in a certain
attitude of the will, is necessarily invisible, and may

---

[1] H. vi. 290. See the summary of this discussion and remarks
upon it in my book called *Problems in the Relations of God and
Man*, pp. 95 foll.

thus demand some visible symbol to bring it vividly before our minds. Thus by *prayer* we may revive our own moral sentiments, by *church-going* we may help to revive those of others, by the custom of *baptism* we may aid in securing the propagation of morality among the next generation, by sacramental *communion* we may do something towards the preservation of the corporate society of religious persons. Of the five ordinances which the Mahommedan religion, says Kant, puts forward as ' means of grace '—washing, praying, fasting, almsgiving, and the pilgrimage to Mecca—in only one besides ' praying ' (which occurs also in his list of Christian ' means of grace '), does Kant find any relation to morality, and even in that only under favourable circumstances. This one is *almsgiving*. Of the four Christian ' means of grace ' (so-called) which he enumerates,—and which are, he adds, to be distinguished from the ' operations of grace' previously discussed in the General Remark at the end of the first section, because in the ' means of grace ' we are not passive but active—the first, *Prayer,* is no more than an uttered wish, acting on us, and not on God, who indeed is better adored in silence since not even the Psalter (he observes) is worthy to express our profound consciousness (a consciousness, as I have often had occasion to observe, notably shared by Kant himself) of the divine wisdom in creation. Indeed of the details of that wisdom the Psalmist (remarks Kant) probably knew but little.

The second so-called 'means of grace', *Church-*

going, is a public duty. From explicit Prayer, which, as we previously saw, Kant thought vanished from men's lives with their progress in virtue and reason, he distinguished the Spirit of Prayer which may always be present and which is meant by ' the prayer without ceasing' recommended by St. Paul.[1] This Spirit, he observes,[2] 'the Teacher of the Gospel has admirably expressed in a formula which makes explicit Prayer and with it itself, as regards its letter, unnecessary'. Under this head he intimates[3] that ' certain acts of adoration addressed to God in the personality of his infinite Goodness under the name of a man' are among formulas which, as tending to idolatry, and so hurtful to the conscience, may constitute a genuine objection to what otherwise might be for a good churchman the public duty of church-going—a duty from which Kant was wont to excuse himself, possibly (though we are not so told) on this very ground. He must here have of course in his mind prayers in the Church service addressed to Christ as God. ' God in the personality of his infinite Goodness' means, as we have seen, for him the second person of the Trinity ;[4] and the worship of this aspect of the divine nature under the name of a man can only refer to the worship of Jesus as the incarnate Son of God. But a ' hymn to Christ as to God' was what struck Pliny in the earliest days of the Church as the characteristic feature of Christian worship ;[5] and it is difficult to think it as easy as not

---

[1] I Thess. v. 17. [2] H. vi. 295 *n.* [3] H. vi. 298.
[4] H. vi. 238. [5] *Ep. ad Trai.* 96.

only Kant but other modern philosophers seem to have done to eliminate this feature from Christianity without destruction of its spiritual identity. On the other hand, it must always be recollected that the central act of Christian worship, the Eucharist, has through all the ages of the Church's history been addressed to the Father only, in the name of the Son. In the same passage we find Kant speaking of the second commandment of the Decalogue, that against idolatry, as a *Vernunftverbote*, a negative command of Reason ; presumably to excuse himself for referring to it as broken in the representation of God as a man, an object of the senses, by claiming for it not merely statutory but rational or intrinsic authority.

The third ordinance reckoned as a 'means of grace' is *Baptism*, a useful and significant ceremony; and the fourth and last is *Communion*, a custom well devised to arouse a sense of fellowship in the universal moral community. But none of them are for Kant 'means of grace' properly so called ; that title must be reserved for the good life alone, which deserves whatever grace God may have in store; about which grace we shall never know any more than just this, that, if it exist, we shall deserve it by a good life.

At this point, before leaving the discussion of this, Kant's principal work on the philosophy of religion, I will add a few very brief remarks on the bearing of his criticism of the notion of Means of Grace upon the theory of Sacraments. Beyond question there is a perpetual danger of the use of sacraments degenerating into magic, wherein it is sought to effect moral and spiritual results by mechanical or physical means : and the abhorrence of any such substitution of the natural for the ethical, which determines Kant's whole treatment of the subject, is a sentiment which it is a real service to religion to keep alive and vigorous.   But unquestionably there are considerations connected with the use of sacraments to which Kant paid insufficient attention.   Even he did not deny that moral sentiments could be stimulated by external social acts, and on this account he allows, as we have seen, a certain utility to the two great Sacraments of the Gospel.   But he fails to recognize that in the undeniable (even if in a certain sense to us inscrutable) connexion between our moral or spiritual life and its physical basis or condition there lies a sanction for the sacramental idea which must not be overlooked. The very being of each of us as person and spirit depends for its original existence upon the purely physical act of generation—an act moreover which is not the act of our individual selves at all.   Our continued existence depends no less on the physical processes of nutrition and digestion ; and no one in practice doubts the influence e.g. of fresh air and of tonics upon our moral sentiments.   It is true that the connexion between the physical acts involved in the use of sacraments and these sentiments is of a different kind, in so far as it is determined not by the laws of physical nature but rather by what we may call psychological laws, so that the cause is to be sought not in the material elements of the sacrament as such, but rather in the convention by which they are taken as symbols. For, although they are selected in virtue of some metaphorical appropriateness to the spiritual effects they are designed to assist in producing, they do not assist in producing it according to natural laws ; and hence the least drop of baptismal water or of eucharistic wine serves its purpose as well as any larger quantity of either. But the effects *do* depend upon the ceremony, and to a ceremony physical acts are as necessary as they are to the communication of thought by speech or writing—a process which offers the closest analogy that we can find to the action of sacraments. The notion of a sacrament undoubtedly involves the recognition of a mediation of the spiritual by the physical which is universally observable, but to the significance of which Kant scarcely pays in his ethics sufficient regard. It should not however be overlooked that the only form of religious sentiment unconnected with our duties to one another of which Kant speaks with respect, and which he would encourage,—it is one by which he himself was strongly affected— namely that of reverence for God's wisdom as evinced in the order of nature, is obviously mediated by that very material system whereof the elements used in sacramental ordinances are a part.

The publication of *Religion within the Limits of mere Reason* not unnaturally brought down upon him the displeasure of the inquisitorial commission which had already attempted to prevent that of the second and third sections : and in 1794 a Cabinet-order was issued, dated October 1, by Wöllner as

Minister, in which the King complained of the book as well as of 'other smaller treatises' as injurious to fundamental doctrines of the Bible and of Christianity, and as inconsistent with the author's duty as an instructor of youth ; and required him, on pain of the royal displeasure, to employ his talents and authority to better purpose. Kant replied [1] in a long defence of himself, couched in very respectful language, but with no withdrawal of anything that he had said ; on the contrary, pointing out that in his academic lectures he had not meddled with the Bible or with Christianity, that the condemned book was not intended as fit for general reading, that it dealt with natural religion and only incidentally and by way of illustration with revealed, and that he had always called attention to the high value of the Bible. He dwelt on the deep sense of responsibility with which he had always written on these subjects, and declared that

'even now in my seventy-first year, when the thought readily suggests itself that I may very likely have shortly to give account of all this before a universal Judge who knows the heart, I can, with all frankness, hand in this answer to the charges against my teaching as made with complete conscientiousness '.

The letter ends however with an act of submission.

'To avoid being blamed in the future for such disfigurement and depreciation of Christianity as has been alleged against me, I hold it the surest way to avoid the least suspicion on that head, most solemnly to declare, as your

[1] H. vii. 325 ff.

Majesty's most faithful subject, that I henceforth will refrain altogether from all public utterances in lectures or in writing on the subject of Religion, whether natural or revealed.'

He added, as he afterwards explained in a work of which I shall speak presently, the words 'as your Majesty's most faithful subject' expressly in order to avoid renouncing for ever his freedom of judgement in this controversy about religion and to limit his promise to the King's lifetime. His biographer Schubert found amid the fragmentary notes which he left behind him the following memorandum, witnessing to the earnest debate with himself which lay behind even this temporary surrender of his claim to free expression of his views.

'To contradict or deny one's inner conviction is contemptible and can be required of no one; but silence, in a case like the present, is the duty of a subject; and if all that one says must be true, it is not therefore one's duty to speak the whole truth openly. I have moreover in that work (*Religion innerhalb der Grenzen des blosen Vernunft*) never added or subtracted a word, nor could I, if I had done so, have hindered my publisher, whose property it is, from printing a second edition. And in my defence the expression I used was intentionally so limited, that in the event of the Monarch dying before me, as I should then become the subject of his successor, I could again enter upon my freedom to think.'

This event did occur in 1797; and the new King, Frederick William III, dismissed Wöllner and abolished the censorship which he had instituted. In the following year Kant published a work called

Der Streit der Facultäten, ' The Controversy between the Faculties ',[1] in the preface to which he published the Cabinet-order of the late Sovereign (of which he had hitherto avoided speaking to friends or colleagues) with his reply thereto ; and, in the body of the work, discussed the relations of philosophy to the three so-called higher faculties of theology, law, and medicine ; a topic which necessarily reopened the question of the right of philosophy to deal with the subject of religion. There is much that is interesting in the discussion ; not however much which for our present purpose throws further light upon his views. He distinguishes true religion as ' that faith which finds the essential feature of all honour paid to God in human morality ' (*in der Moralität der Menschen*) from ' heathenism ', which does not find it there. Every ' Church faith ' has, he thinks, ' a certain admixture of heathenism ', namely an element of external, statutable worship, over and above the purely ethical. He looks forward to a closing scene of the great drama of religious change on earth, when Judaism (leaving aside all its positive doctrines, whereof some, he observes, still remain even in Christianity, in connexion with the notion of Jesus as the Jewish Messiah) shall find its euthanasia in that pure moral religion to which Christianity has so far most closely approximated, and ' there shall be one flock and one shepherd '.[2] He contrasts two doctrines of conversion, that of the Pietism of Spener and Franck, and that of the

[1] H. vii. 321 foll.   [2] John x. 16.

Moravian movement inaugurated by Zinzendorf. According to the former, conversion begins in a breach with sin, which is only possible through a miracle, but ends in a morally good course of life according to Reason. According to the latter, the original change of disposition from evil to good happens naturally through the perception of our sinfulness in view of the moral law held up to us by Reason, but continuance in the good disposition is only possible through constant communion of a supernatural kind with the Divine Spirit. Both of these views appear to Kant tinged with fanaticism ; the former as implying the power of distinguishing the operation of Grace from that of natural Reason, the latter as relying upon supposed supernatural experience and excited feelings. He recognizes however that both kinds of ' Reason-slaying Mysticism ' have in them something which is lacking to what he calls ' soulless orthodoxy ', the doctrine of an infallible book. The true mean between them lies in the Biblical doctrine interpreted by the Practical Reason working in the hearts of all men in the direction of a fundamental improvement of moral disposition, and uniting them in a universal but invisible Church. He does not (any more than did the ancient Alexandrians) despise the use of the allegorical interpretation of Scripture in the service and interest of Reason ; it serves, he remarks, as a protection against such fantastic mysticism as Swedenborg's. The Government must not let the Bible be discredited. But we cannot allow that a doctrine is of God because it is in the Bible; we must take it for our principle that it is in the Bible because it is of God. This principle is indeed not capable of proof; *supernaturalium non datur scientia*. But there must be in any national religion some kind of standard of doctrine; and this justifies us in treating the Bible, with its well-proved power of planting religion in men's hearts, as the ' word of God '; but only as interpreted by the Practical Reason, which is in the last resort God's sole authentic communication to man. ' The God ', he says,[1] ' who speaks through our own Practical Reason is an infallible and universally comprehensible interpreter of this word of his and there can indeed be no other, since Religion is a matter of pure Reason.'

To the portion of the work now before us devoted to the relation of the theological Faculty to the philosophical Kant appends [2] an interesting note taken from a work by a certain Wilmans, who had written a dissertation *de similitudine inter mysticismum purum et Kantianam religionis doctrinam*, published at Halle in 1797. This dissertation contained an account of a class of men known to him ' who are called Separatists but call themselves Mystics '; mostly tradesmen, manual workers, agricultural labourers, though with one or two gentlemen and scholars among them, accepting indeed the Bible as of divine origin, but interpreting it by its agreement with the law written on their hearts; dispensing altogether with external divine worship, yet (apart

[1] H. vii. 384.   [2] H. vii. 386 foll.

from some black sheep) exemplary in their lives : resembling the Quakers, except that they wear no peculiar dress, and pay without demur all dues, civil and ecclesiastical ; ' true Kantians, were they philosophers ' ; such of them as are educated, free from all fanaticism, using their powers of reasoning and judgement freely and without prejudice on matters of religion. By his inclusion of Wilmans's account of these people in the text of his book Kant seems to have welcomed them as exhibiting in practice the principles he would recommend to the Christian Church in general.

With the *Streit der Facultäten* I end my account (which however might well be fuller) of the treatment accorded by Kant in the works published in his lifetime to the problems of the philosophy of religion. But before passing to the *Opus Postumum* I will recapitulate very briefly what seem to me the salient features of his teaching, as it has so far come before us.

> Two things there are that fill the mind with awe,
> The starry heavens and our sense of law.

So some one has (rather cumbrously) versified in English the famous words in the concluding section of the *Critique of Practical Reason* :[1] ' Two things fill the mind with ever new and increasing amazement and reverent awe, the oftener and the more steadily our thoughts occupy themselves with them ; the starry Heaven above me, and the Moral Law within me—*der bestirnte Himmel über mir, und das moralische*

[1] H. v. 167.

Gesetz in mir.' These last words are graven over Kant's tomb in the cathedral of Königsberg, and they may well serve as a text to any reflections on his philosophy of religion. Wordsworth, probably not uninfluenced by Kant through Coleridge, has brought the two objects of our reverence mentioned by the philosopher into a closer union in his great *Ode to Duty* :

> Thou dost preserve the stars from wrong,
> And the most ancient heavens through thee are fresh
> and strong.

But the mutual relation of the two grand stimulants of religious sentiment—for so we may properly call them—which were thus recognized by Kant is never made by him as clear as we could wish. This fact, which has an important bearing on the development of his thought on the subject of religion, forces itself on any one who surveys that development as exhibited in his writings.[1]

We know from a passage of Kant's *Nachlass*[2] that he regarded himself as converted by the study of Rousseau from his original attitude as a scientific inquirer, looking down on the uneducated multitude, and regarding the attainment of theoretical or speculative truth as the chief end of human existence, to the recognition of the moral capacity in all men, uneducated as well as educated, to be determined by the law of duty to will and act in accordance there-

---

[1] I observe that it is emphasized in a recent essay on ' Kant und die Religion ', by Prof. Stephan of Halle, included in the *Jubiläumsheft* of the *Kantstudien*, pp. 207 foll.   [2] H. viii. 624.

with, as that part of their nature wherein resided the true dignity of humanity. In other words he passed to the recognition of the primacy of the Practical Reason, concerned as it is with the whole of our personal activity, over the Theoretical Reason, the interest of which is necessarily the concern of a few, and constitutes even for these only a department of their life. More or less simultaneously with this revival in him, under the influence of Rousseau, of the sympathy with uncultured goodness and of the moral earnestness which had no doubt been implanted in him in his earliest years by his home life and his Pietistic education, there was going on in his mind the progress from Dogmatism to Criticism, to use his own expression, which made him come increasingly to distrust the pretensions of the scientific understanding to establish by a process of reasoning the existence of a God, the proper object of a rational being's religious veneration. His reaction under the influence of Rousseau, with its democratic tendency, against the narrowly intellectual attitude which he has described as having been his own, and which was natural enough to a youth of extraordinary powers of mind, raised by education above his original humble surroundings, and joyfully escaped from the emotionally devout atmosphere of his Pietistic schooldays into the freedom of the mathematical and scientific class-rooms of the University, combined with his growing discontent with the arguments for God's existence then current in the schools to encourage him to seek in the Moral

Law an object for the sentiment of religious veneration which was always a marked feature of his
character. For he felt himself by no means released
from the obligation of that law by his loss of con-
fidence in arguments which, after all, had never
claimed to establish the being of a *moral* God, but
only that of an intelligent creator, a necessary being,
or a sum total of reality. But, while he ceased not to
regard a reference to 'design' as ultimately necessary
to *explain* to ourselves the origin at any rate of
organic nature, whether it were really the ground of it
or no ; and still less ceased to *believe* in the Creator
whose existence he had come to consider theoretically
indemonstrable ; his conception of this Creator
came to be not less but more *transcendent*, in the
sense that the reference to him of the order of nature
became something neither evident nor even capable
of being inferred from phenomena, but a mere
'regulative idea', indispensable perhaps, but with
no claim to be taken for metaphysical truth, although
negatively valuable as ruling out alternatives which,
in a region necessarily beyond the ken of our intelligence, would accord less well with the facts
within our ken. On the other hand, the God whose
voice was heard by Kant in the Moral Law tended
to become in his thought more and more *immanent* ;
for this God could not be conceived without injury
to our whole moral outlook as accessible otherwise
than *through* the moral law. We might indeed with
advantage represent what our conscience perceives
of itself to be right, not merely as the commands of

our own reason, but as those of God ; but only on condition of seeing in God no other than a Reason identical with our own, as ours is with that of all rational beings, yet untrammelled by having associated with it a sensitive nature with its self-regarding appetites and peculiar point of view.

It would not be true to say that Kant did not occupy himself at all with the problem of the relation between the God to whom our heart was uplifted in reverent worship by the spectacle of the starry heavens and the God who is one with our moral reason. He did not doubt that they were one God. In his so-called moral argument for God's existence in the *Critique of Practical Reason* [1] he attempted to see in their unity the solution of the apparent discrepancy between that which is and that which ought to be ; the 'ought' of the moral law guaranteeing the actuality of a being capable of realizing its demands by ordering the natural world in accordance therewith. In the *Kritik der Urtheilskraft* he suggested [2] the profounder thought that only the recognition of the absolute value of the morally good will can provide a firm basis for any teleology, by giving us an adequate end of the existence of the world and all that is in it ; a recognition which, though in itself independent of any perception of purposiveness in nature, is, as it were, confirmed by the hints thereof which we find in organisms, which we cannot explain to ourselves except through the conception of purposiveness. These

[1] H. v. 130 foll.   [2] H. v. 455 foll.

attempts to unite the two revelations of God which Kant found in nature and in the soul respectively may seem inconclusive and unsatisfactory ; but there can be no question that Kant united them in his own religious life, venerating, with Wordsworth, as he gazed at the starry heavens, the same God that speaks within us in the moral law.

I have already suggested however that it is to be regretted, from the point of view of the theory of Religion, that Kant did not more clearly perceive in his own attitude in the presence of the starry heavens a proof that Religion has other roots than the experience of moral obligation. The perception of this truth need not really have interfered with his insistence, which has been so important in the history of European theology, on the impossibility of justifying the use of the conception of God in the exposition of the truth about Nature without any reference to the moral and religious experience of mankind, apart from which our conception of God would not have lain ready to the hand of philosophers at all. And it might have checked to some extent a tendency which the later adventures of theology, especially in the school of Ritschl and in other circles standing more particularly under Kant's influence, have shown to exist—a tendency to repeat the mistake of the ancient Marcionite heresy, against which Tertullian wrote, by separating the God to whom our moral consciousness points us from the Power revealed in the world as known to science and the Unity which is the object of the philosopher's quest.

VI

KANT'S PHILOSOPHY OF RELIGION: THE *OPUS POSTUMUM*

Of late attention has been called to the fragmentary work which was found after Kant's death among his papers, some very arbitrarily chosen selections from which were published forty years ago by Reicke, but of which the appearance of a much more full account by Professor Adickes four years ago has now enabled us to form a more adequate judgement. A valuable description of it, as edited by Adickes, and a discussion of the question how far it indicates a real change in Kant's views, will be found in the third appendix to the second edition of Professor Kemp Smith's *Commentary on the Critique of Pure Reason.* The change has been held to extend to a denial that God is more than what we may call a methodological fiction. We have now to ask whether the material put at our disposal by Adickes will justify us in taking this view of it; and again whether, short of this, it amounts (as has also, I believe, been suggested) to a complete surrender by Kant of the thought of a transcendent Deity, and a transition to a pure Immanentism, such as we have seen in our study of his earlier writings to have been so little attractive to him that he seems scarcely able to enter into the position of such a philosopher as Spinoza with sufficient sympathy even to criticize it to any purpose.

It appears that the portion of the *Opus Postumum* which concerns us mostly here was written by Kant (who died in 1804) in the years 1800–3, when he was greatly interested in a certain book by Lichtenberg, a physicist who had studied Kant's published works, and who, as I gather from Professor Kemp Smith,[1]—I have not read him at first hand—attempted a reconciliation of his philosophy with Spinoza's, interest in which, as I remarked before, had by this time been, after a long period of neglect, revived by Goethe and his contemporaries.

I mentioned before, in speaking of Kant's attitude toward Spinoza, the curious fact that in the *Opus Postumum* he constantly confuses with him a very different although nearly contemporary philosopher, Malebranche, attributing to the former the celebrated phrase of the latter about 'seeing all things in God', the true authorship of which he had known when he wrote his Inaugural Dissertation some twenty years before. The expression could hardly have found a place in Spinoza ; but, as Adickes says,[2] Kant had probably in his mind a dim recollection of Spinoza's *res sub aeternitatis specie contemplari*.[3] Kant does not understand by the ' seeing all things in God ' what it is in Malebranche, a theory of sense-perception, but the unification of all the formal elements of

[1] *Commentary*, 2nd. ed., p. 635.   [2] p. 762.
[3] *Eth.* ii. 44, coroll. II.

our knowledge under a single principle. The enthusiasm of the above-mentioned Lichtenberg for Spinoza seems to have disposed Kant to think more sympathetically of the latter than he had formerly done. The view that a purified Christianity for people without philosophical training as the best available surrogate for a pure religion of reason, which Lichtenberg is quoted by Adickes [1] as putting forward, is of course thoroughly Kantian ; but Lichtenberg identifies the pure religion of reason with Spinozism, and this would tend to recommend Spinozism to Kant.

But Kant's thought does not even now really move on the same lines as Spinoza's ; the apparent approximation does not go beyond a greater emphasis on divine immanence than we find before. There was indeed nothing new to Kant in the view that the divine Reason and Will expressed in the Moral Law is not other than our own ; and that it is only as being our own that it possesses for us the ' manifest authority ' (to use Butler's phrase) [2] which belongs to it.

But he constantly dwells in the *Opus Postumum* on the self-creating activity of the Reason as a source of ideas, and of a complete system of these ; it is implied that the creation in *Genesis* is but a mythical representation of this activity. The phrase *sichselbst konstituieren* constantly recurs ; and it is used both of man and of God ; God is said to ' constitute himself a Person ' ; and the highest Will

---

[1] p. 763.   [2] *Sermon* II.

to 'constitute itself the highest Being as *ens summum, summa intelligentia, summum bonum* '.[1]

Man too is 'his own maker and originator according to the quality of Personality ' ;[2] that is, Personality, and indeed all spiritual perfection, is represented, not only in man but in God, not as something just *there*, given to start with, but rather as the result of free activity. A Person is defined as ' a Being determining itself according to principles of Freedom'.[3] 'Among all properties', it is said, 'which belong to a thinking Being, the first is the property of being conscious of himself as a Person, according to which the Subject, according to Transcendental Idealism, constitutes itself its Object *a priori* ' :[4] and again, ' A rational being, in so far as it personifies itself for the sake of an end, is a moral Person '.[5]

It is interesting to observe that in the *Opus Postumum* Kant constantly (with whatever meaning,—we will consider this later) speaks of God as a 'Person' and of God's 'Personality'. I have elsewhere shown [6] —before I became acquainted with Kant's *Opus Postumum*—how rare this language is before the end of the eighteenth century. The traditional use of ' Person ' in respect of God had in view the personal distinctions within the Godhead affirmed by the doctrine of the Trinity ; and even the Socinians who taught that there was only *one* Person in God had done this rather by way of denying that there were *three* than with any desire to insist upon Personality

[1] pp. 766, 772.   [2] p. 767.   [3] p. 768.
[4] Ibid.   [5] Ibid.   [6] *God and Personality*, p. 62 f.

as a divine attribute. In Kant's own earlier writings
we shall look in vain for an ascription of Personality
to God ; but here in the *Opus Postumum* it constantly recurs. At first, at any rate, the fact is
surprising. It does not appear, from anything said
by Professor Adickes, that any of the books which
seem to have been influencing Kant at the time
suggested the expression to his mind. Moreover,
since, later on in the nineteenth century, the expression ' Personality of God ' (which I find first in
Paley and in Schleiermacher) became usual, insistence on it has generally been the mark of a theology
of *transcendence*, rather than of *immanence* ; here,
however, in these latest lucubrations of Kant's, it goes
along with a greater disposition to a doctrine of
divine immanence than had appeared in his previous
books. We will see what further light, if any, our
subsequent quotations will throw upon this unexpected feature of the last phase of his thought.

A Person is, according to Kant here, a rational
being with rights ; if he has duties too, he is a man ;
if not, he is God.[1] Once it is said that a Person is a
rational being with rights and no duties ;[2] this would
ascribe, as Adickes says, Personality to God and *not*
to man. One is at first inclined to wonder whether
this statement can really have been intended and is
not only a slip. But it is true that even in earlier
writings, and certainly in the *Opus Postumum*, it
is rather with the legislative capacity of Reason in
us than with our subordination to Reason, which

---

[1] p. 773.   [2] Ibid.

rests upon our possession of a recalcitrant sensibility and involves the appearance of moral necessity in our lives under the guise of obligation, the imposition on us of a duty in opposition to our natural inclination, that Kant associates our title to Personality. Thus we might expect to find Personality attributed to God, who is conceived as Sovereign and not Subject in the Kingdom of Ends (*we* are both), as more properly belonging to him than to men. But previously to the *Opus Postumum* Kant avoids, whether deliberately or not, such a way of speaking. In the *Opus Postumum* however we find a decided tendency to define *Person* and *Persönlichkeit* in a fashion which makes them specially applicable to the divine as distinguished from the human spirit ; in a context, however, we must remember, which exhibits a more marked leaning than is apparent in Kant's earlier works to emphasis on the identity of the human spirit, when fully in possession of its rational freedom, with the divine. ' Person ' is a ' substance consciously fitted to all ends ' (*allen Zwecken mit Bewusstsein angemessen*),[1] and again, ' a being of pure intelligence ' (*reines Verstandeswesen*).[2]

Persönlichkeit, again, is equated in one place with ' a spontaneous power of causality to determine itself ' and in reference to its effects to originate commands to nature ' *ursprünglich über die Natur gebietend zu sein* ' ;[3] and in another with the ' sublime quality in Freedom itself of being itself an originating cause '.[4] Clearly, if God is to be distinguished from

---

[1] p. 773. [2] Ibid. [3] Ibid. [4] Ibid.

man at all, it is rather to God than to man that Personality, thus defined or described, would properly be ascribed.

We shall then be desirous to know what Kant has to say of the relation of God to man ; and on this subject we learn that God cannot give men a good will ; he cannot, though holy himself, create holy beings ; only so far as they are natural beings is he the creator of men ; as moral beings they are their own creators.[1] There is in principle nothing in this inconsistent with Kant's earlier views. I suggested in my Gifford Lectures,[2] and still think it probable, that the very expression *Reich* in the phrase usually translated as ' Kingdom of Ends ' connoted to Kant, as *Reich* would naturally connote to him, not a monarchy like that of Prussia in his time, which was a *Königreich* not a *Reich*, but a State like the Holy Roman Empire, to which alone the title was in his day applied in Germany, wherein the Emperor, though differing from the other princes in having no superior, was by no means sovereign over them as they were over their own subjects ; his supremacy being rather the expression of the common law which, among all the diversities of territorial enactments, ran throughout the Empire, and was the source of their own sovereign authority. God is thus Sovereign as we are not, because the moral law is not imposed upon him, as it is upon us, to be obeyed against natural inclination, but is rather the

[1] p. 774.
[2] *Divine Personality and Human Life*, p. 128.

expression of a will which no animal nature resists and no evil bias perverts ; whereas in us there are both these impediments to the free activity of practical Reason which are absent in him.

Man must therefore be the author of his own good will and man who has attained pure moral goodness cannot be the originator of his own corruption ; 'he who originally makes himself evil is' (not man but) ' devil '.[1] Adickes notes that elsewhere the assertion of the existence of such an Evil Principle is rejected as a *contradictio in adjecto*.[2] But, though without the MS. before one, one is at a disadvantage in criticizing the statements cited, I do not see anything here which is not easily explained by a reference to *Religion innerhalb der Grenzen der blossen Vernunft*. The notion of a *devil* is that of a being with an evil disposition not due, as man's is, to a radical perversion, or 'original sin', which although imputed as his own act, since it repeats itself in every man as a free choice, is yet ingrained in his nature as man. But how the Devil himself, not having this evil propensity, could fall is wholly inscrutable ; and the introduction of the Devil into our account of the origin of sin has purely the negative significance of contrasting with our position another, conceivable or at least conjecturable, with which it must not be confused ; it in no way enlarges our knowledge of supersensible reality. Nothing in the passages cited by Adickes from the *Opus Postumum* appears to be inconsistent with this. The mythology

[1] p. 774. [2] Ibid.

B b

which Kant interprets is of course that which makes the Devil's own fall antecedent not only to man's fall, but to man's creation; as it is represented, for example, in *Paradise Lost*. This is what we find in Augustine, who attributes it to a perversion of will, whose origin is itself inscrutable.[1] Professor Burkitt has lately suggested [2] that this theory, which differs from those which make the Devil's fall subsequent to man's creation (e. g. that which identified it with the illicit intercourse of the Watchers with daughters of men, or the Mahommedan explanation of it as due to refusal on his part to worship Adam), is traceable to the Manichean theory with which Augustine was familiar during the period in which he himself was a Manichee.

God, according to Kant in the *Opus Postumum*, is said to be neither World Soul nor Demiurge; [3] although in another passage [4] the latter title is allowed him so far as he is regarded as exercising an unrestricted power over nature; but not so far as he is thought of with reference to the freedom of rational beings, where he is a *holy* Being, not the creator, strictly speaking, of moral agents but their *ideal*. The meaning of this distinction is, of course, in harmony with the mature Kantian view. In respect of Nature, God is merely inferred as the purposive Mind, without the assumption of which we cannot explain organic nature; a more positive conception of his relation to the world is beyond our grasp;

---

[1] *De Civ. Dei*, xii. 7.
[2] *Religion of the Manichees*, p. 102 f.   [3] p. 774.   [4] Ibid.

and this negative or merely regulative notion of it is based on our inability to dispense with it, rather than on any speculative value of its own. On the other hand, though, even in the sphere of morality, our thought of God has not the character of knowledge, yet we have a positive interest in denying him to be related to us in any such way as would impair our own moral freedom ; and hence in denying him to be the creator of our moral disposition. So far we have nothing in the *Opus Postumum* inconsistent with what our previous study of Kant would have led us to expect.

When Kant enters more particularly into the reasons for rejecting the two designations of Demiurge and of World Soul as applicable to God, we find expressions indicating that he was now inclined to regard the natural world as, when taken by itself, suggesting its origin from a non-moral or even immoral intelligence. Adickes [1] sees here a stark pessimism in respect of the empirical course of the world, strengthened in the ageing Kant by the experience of a long life, and compares the mention of an evil soul or souls by the side of the good World Soul in Plato's last work, the *Laws*.[2] I do not deny that this interpretation may be placed upon the passages in question. But a distinct tendency to pessimism is found in Kant long before this ; and it is notorious that Schopenhauer, a Kantian (in intention at any rate) who rejected his master's ethical doctrine of obligation, found Kant's

[1] p. 775.   [2] x. 896 E seq.

philosophy—quite apart from the *Opus Postumum*—serve very well as a background to his own pessimistic system. The whole development of Kant's theology had (despite his personal sense of religious awe in the presence of the starry heavens and of the wisdom manifested in the instinctive actions of animals) been steadily in the direction of minimizing the use of the idea of God in physics and metaphysics, wherein it had with the great thinkers of the seventeenth century played so considerable a part, and of finding in our moral experience the sole *source* of the idea, even when once suggested there it might be allowed to afford as a clue for the interpretation of certain facts in nature. The more trenchant expressions of the *Opus Postumum* harmonize with this general tendency of his thought, while we must bear in mind that we do not know that he would necessarily have committed himself to them in this form, had the work he had in hand reached the stage at which he would have given it to the world.

To the description of God as the World Soul Kant objects [1] as making him a hypothetical being supposed to account for empirical facts, like the caloric or elastic fluid, invented by the physicists of his day to account for the phenomena of heat ; whereas *die moralisch-praktisch Vernunft*, the morally practical Reason, is the only true source of the conception. It is interesting to note here the congruity of Kant's teaching with a tradition of Christian

[1] pp. 775, 776.

theology to which it is very unlikely that his attention had ever been called. The correspondence of the Spirit as the third person of the Christian Trinity with the World Soul of the triad of divine ὑποστάσεις developed by the neo-Platonists out of the hints afforded in Plato's *Timaeus* is obvious ; and in the twelfth century the allegation by Abelard [1] of statements in the later pagan writers (such as Macrobius) [2] about the *Anima Mundi* as proof of an agreement in principle with the Christian doctrine of God was one of the venturesome sayings of that great man which called down upon him the suspicion of the watchful heresy-hunter St. Bernard.[3] Whatever we may think of the latter's controversial temper and methods, it must be admitted that something more than mere words was at stake in this question of the identity or otherwise of the Holy Spirit of Christian doctrine with the Platonic Soul of the World. It is I think on the whole true to say that theological tradition had usually assigned rather to the Logos, the second person of the Trinity, ' by whom all things consist',[4] the function of upholding the world, while the Spirit was always closely associated with the Church and the special revelation of God therein.

In his recent book on *The Holy Spirit and the Church* [5] Bishop Gore has pointed out that this is

---

[1] *Introd. ad Theol.* (*Opp.* ed. Cousin, ii. 49 seq.).
[2] *Comm. in Somn. Scip.* i. 14.
[3] *Tract. de Erroribus Abaelardi*, c. 4, § 10.
[4] Col. i. 17.   [5] c. i.

the case in the New Testament itself in contrast
with the Old. The regular use of the expression
' Holy Spirit ' is here significant ; for this implies
that the activity specially ascribed to the Spirit
is a sanctifying activity, that is to say an activity
directed to the wills of beings standing in moral
relations with their fellows, rather than one directed
to the world which we call *natural* precisely in order
to distinguish it from the contrasted sphere of freedom, of morality, and of society. Now Kant, quite
in harmony with this tradition, lays stress upon
holiness as the special characteristic of God as revealed through the Moral Law, and objects to the
description of him as the World Soul on the ground
that it is not in the world revealed to us by the
sciences (where he only appears as a despot) but in
our consciousness of the Moral Law that we become
aware of this holiness as expressing his true character.
In other words, he agrees with Bernard against
Abelard in refusing to equate the Holy Spirit with
the *Anima Mundi* ; and it is noteworthy that Abelard
himself, in saying, as he does, that the Holy Spirit
may be called *Anima Mundi, id est universorum
fidelium vitam atque salutem,*[1] may be said to draw the
sting of his own identification.

But the reality of God, not as World Soul, nor
as the Creator inferred from his creation, but as the
imponent of the Moral Law, had become more
evident to Kant in this last stage of his life than
ever. 'What is God ?' 'Is there a God ?' he asks ;

[1] *Introd. ad Theol.* (*Opp*. ed. Cousin, ii. 37).

and he answers : [1] ' In the world considered as a
totality of rational beings, there is also a totality
of morally practical Reason, and consequently of
an imperative Right (*Rechtsimperativ*) and therewith
also a God.' If I understand this not very clearly
expressed sentence correctly, he conceives God to
be revealed in the Moral Law ' taken as a whole ',
in virtue of their common subjection to which all
rational beings form a single whole or community
such as he elsewhere had described as a Kingdom of
Ends. He says also : [2] ' The mere Idea of God is at
the same time (*zugleich*) the proof of his existence ' ;
and again : [3] ' The mere Idea of God is at the same
time (*zugleich*) a Postulate of his existence ' (that
is, I suppose, postulates his existence). ' To think
of him and to believe in him is an identical act.' [4]
Once more : ' The thought of God is at the same
time (*zugleich*) belief in him and in his Personality.' [5]
These passages suggest an attitude towards God
differing in a very interesting way from that to which
we are accustomed in the earlier writings of Kant.
There we feel, as I have several times remarked, that
the emotion aroused in him by the thought of the
Moral Law was in the truest sense religious ; but
that ' the representation of its precepts as divine
commands ', which, according to him, constituted
Religion, did not in any sense enhance the religious
character of this emotion ; rather, by at once, on the
one hand, suggesting the difficulties of reconciling
the demands of morality with the facts of experience,

[1] p. 776.   [2] Ibid.   [3] Ibid.   [4] Ibid.   [5] Ibid.

and, on the other, arousing Kant's never-sleeping dread of self-delusion through imagining God as present in a quasi-sensible fashion, it introduced a note of criticism and hesitation which tended to render it more doubtful.   Kant, then, at that time still found his religious sentiments powerfully aroused (though he does not *call* them religious in this case) by the spectacle of the divine Wisdom revealed in Nature apart from the Moral Law.   But now his sense of this manifestation of God in Nature seems clouded by a doubt, not only of its theoretical certainty, but of the *goodness* of the Power thus revealed ; on the other hand, the divine origin of the Moral Law is no longer a mere manner of representing it, with which one may dispense without necessarily affecting our consciousness of *its* own majesty; this divine origin is immediately revealed in the Law itself.   In recognizing the Law we find ourselves in God's presence ; and the language of personal intercourse is no longer forbidden us as involving an inadmissible severance of God from his Law; for the Law itself *is* the revelation of his Personality.   Such at least seems to me to be what these citations from the *Opus Postumum* suggest ; a consciousness of God, which, just because he is no longer *transcendent* after the fashion of the older deism, is, in a way in which it was not before, describable as the consciousness of a *personal* God.

'Reason proceeds', says Kant in another note,[1] ' according to the categorical imperative, and the

[1] p. 778.

lawgiver is God.   There is a God, for there is a
Categorical Imperative.' The consciousness of moral
Freedom, he declares, ' is the feeling of the presence
of the Godhead in man '.[1]

Without any knowledge of the *Opus Postumum*,
Adickes's account of which was then unpublished,
I observed in 1920 [2] that Kant, while coming very
near to, had notwithstanding never reached the conclusion which was, as I contended, legitimately to be
drawn from that consciousness of moral obligation
which no one has felt more profoundly and described
more accurately than he; the conclusion stated by
Martineau in these words : ' In the act of conscience
we are immediately introduced to the Higher than
ourselves that gives us what we feel.' [3]   In the *Opus
Postumum* I think we may say that he does reach
that conclusion.

Among the sentences set down by Kant on the
subject of our knowledge of God in the sheets
published as the *Opus Postumum* there are some
which make it impossible, I think, to suppose that
Kant had completely clarified and reduced his
philosophy to a consistent system.   This, which he
had never succeeded in doing in his earlier days, it
is very unlikely that he would have been able to
accomplish in these last years of failing vigour.   Accordingly we find [4] in the immediate neighbourhood
of assertions that the divine nature, except as regards
its moral attributes, is wholly inscrutable to us,

---

[1] Ibid.   [2] *Divine Personality and Human Life*, p. 123.
[3] *Study of Religion*, ii. 27.   [4] p. 780.

the declaration that ' in him, that is through his all-enabling bringing of the world into existence (*sein allvermögendes Werde der Welt*), we live and move and have our being ; God and the world are not co-ordinate (as body and soul), but the one is sub-ordinate to the other ; and the Spirit that makes these forces active does not stand to the world as the soul to an animal, but as the quickening Spirit of material nature in general '. I do not say that Kant could not have harmonized the doctrine of this passage with the affirmation that the Moral Law is the revelation of God which alone makes possible a recognition of his activity in nature ; but un-doubtedly we have before us rather the juxtaposition of different points of view than a synthesis of them in a unified system. What seems to be in Kant's mind is the conviction that the relation of the order of nature to the God revealed to conscience *might* be and, in view of the ultimate unity postulated by the very nature of our intelligence, *must* be that of a material system to the source of its motion, but could not be that of the body of an animal to its soul. Students of ancient philosophy will observe that in this point Kant would have stood on the whole with Aristotle against Plato, although nothing could be less Aristotelian than his principal doctrine of the Moral Law as the supreme and only direct revelation of God to man.

We have previously noted that Kant had already (in the *Critique of Practical Reason*) tended to identify our personality with the autonomous will in us, and so with the Moral Law in which that will is expressed. Thus he could speak of reverence as due to persons only ;[1] and as he also in the same work refers to the 'solemn majesty' of the Moral Law (*seine feierliche Majestät*) as the supreme object of our reverence,[2] one would infer that he even then regarded the Moral Law as personal, although not speaking of it as God's immediate presence in our souls so plainly as he does in the *Opus Postumum*. He preferred to regard it, as I said, as *our* personality. Indeed he speaks in one place[3] of the human *person*, when regarded as belonging to the world of sense, being subject to his own *personality* so far as that belongs to the intelligible world ; and so bound to treat it, though his own essence, 'with nothing short of respect, and its laws with the highest reverence'. In such passages as this we have anticipated, I think, everything in the doctrine of the *Opus Postumum* except the direct identification of this highest factor in our nature with God ; and even this is implied in the view of God as being Sovereign in the Kingdom of Ends, not because its law expresses his will as distinct from that of the subjects in that realm and impressed upon them from without, but because, although that law derives its authority over them from the fact that it expresses their *own* will, this same will is regarded as existing in God pure and unresisted by any recalcitrant element, such as that sensibility in regard to which the will expressed in the Moral Law, though our

[1] H. v. 81. [2] H. v. 82. [3] H. v. 91.

own, presents itself as though it were another than ours. I thus do not find any really new doctrine in the *Opus Postumum*, but still the language is not quite the same as that of earlier works. The following citations however will show that Kant, while more ready to speak of God as directly present in our moral experience, is as much in earnest as ever in denying any such distinction between God and his law as would justify either the inclusion in the latter of any arbitrary or merely statutory element or a corresponding possibility of access to God otherwise than through the law itself. ' God is not ', he says in one of Adickes's citations,[1] ' a Being outside of me, but merely a thought within me. God is the morally practical Reason giving laws to itself. One God, in me, around me, and above me.' And in another,[2] ' The proposition, There is a God, means no more than : There is in human reason, determining itself according to morality, a supreme Principle which perceives itself determined and necessitated to act without cessation in accordance with such a Principle.' And, once more,[3] ' God must only be sought *within* us '. We cannot but be reminded here of the Pauline teaching [4] about ' the righteousness which is of faith ', which ' speaketh on this wise : Say not in thine heart Who shall ascend into heaven (that is, to bring down Christ from above), or Who shall descend into the deep (that is, to bring up Christ again from the dead) ; but what saith it ? The word is nigh unto thee, even in thy mouth and in thy heart.'

[1] p. 819.   [2] Ibid.   [3] Ibid.   [4] Rom. x. 6 ff.

In this identification of the divine Presence with the Moral Law Kant seemed to himself to have reconciled the demand of the religious consciousness for a present object of worship with the rejection of any idolatrous and fantastic attempt to apprehend the divine Presence by the senses. 'There is a God,' he declares,[1] 'for there is a Categorical Imperative of Duty, before which all knees do bow, whether they be in heaven or in the earth or under the earth ; and whose Name is holy, without our having to suppose a substance which represents this Being to the senses.'

'In it,' another passage tells us,[2] 'that is in the idea of God as a moral Being, we live and move and have our being, impelled by the recognition of our duties as divine commands. The conception of God is the idea of a moral Being which, passing judgement in accordance with moral principles, exercises universal authority. This is not a hypothetical thing, but the pure practical Reason itself in its personality, and with executive powers in relation to the system of the world and its forces.' He sometimes however wavers in his use of language. At least in one place quoted by Adickes [3] he seems to say expressly that *personality* is not to be attributed to God ; the context however suggests that here the older thought has come back, which he had not at all rejected, that God is not a person distinct from our own autonomous practical Reason confronting us in the Moral Law. He states the matter very clearly in another

[1] p. 820.   [2] p. 821.   [3] p. 822.

sentence,[1] where he declares that in all good actions, actions done that is from duty, the authoritative element in the act,—which is not *our* goodwill towards the persons who are benefited by them, but the *right* in those persons merely as men, which is fulfilled by the actions in question—is ascribed to God as an ideal *person*, but *not* as a substance distinct from man. ' There is ', he says,[2] ' a Being in me, distinguished from myself as the cause of an effect wrought upon me, which freely—that is without being dependent on laws of nature in space and time—judges me within, justifying or condemning me ; and I as man am myself this being, and it is no substance external to me, and—what is most surprising of all—its causality is no natural necessity but a determination of me to a free act.'

Again : [3] ' God is thus no substance discoverable outside of me but merely a moral relation within me.' And in a passage which breaks off abruptly before the sentence is complete : [4] ' the idea (*Idee*)—not conception (*Begriff*)—of God is not the conception of a substance. The Personality which we attribute to it, which is also bound up with the unity of this object (not many gods) ....' Here Kant seems to have been struck with the thought that there is a close connexion between the *unity* of God, which is the essential unity of the Moral Law, identical for all rational beings, and the denial to him of the kind of imagined ' personality ' which would render possible the thought of other such persons beside this one.

[1] p. 823.   [2] p. 824.   [3] p. 826.   [4] Ibid.

This seems to be implied in the following citation : [1] ' The idea of that which the human Reason itself makes of the universe '—I suppose he means as the field of the operations of the moral Reason—' is the active representation (*aktive Vorstellung*) of God, not as the substance of a *separate* personality outside of me, but as the thought of a personality within me ' ; and in this : [2] ' God is a power commanding us through a Categorical Imperative without reference to our happiness (*Wohlbefinden*); a real Person, but certainly not one perceptible as an object of the senses.'

This is a *prima vindemiatio* from the *Opus Postumum*, and I will now try to describe the impression it has made on myself. It is the impression of the aged Kant interested in the Spinozism of the generation which had arisen since his own, and trying to see how his own convictions, the fruit of long mental travail, stood in relation to it ; interested too in the recently published accounts of Zoroastrianism, a religion whereof the strict theme seemed to be, as of his own chief work on the subject, the contest of the Good and Evil Principles for dominion over men; so that he even tried to see how *Zoroaster* would look as the title of his own projected work ; as little disposed as ever to a merely naturalistic immanentism, but less reluctant to express his profound reverence for the Moral Law in religious language, as reverence for the Presence of God therein immediately revealed ; and, finally, attracted by the thought that,

[1] p. 827.　　　　　[2] p. 828.

after all, in such a revelation God was more truly revealed as *personal* than when imaginatively represented as external to our own inner and essential life ; for he is now *our own personality*, confronting us as the ideal realized by us in so far as we exhibit the good disposition which alone constitutes any moral worth whereunto we can pretend. Here is no *Schwärmerei*, but a religion of pure morality, whose God is no conjectured Cause to account for phenomena, nor even a personification of the Moral Law, which we conveniently may, though we need not of necessity, employ ; but a Presence ' closer to us than breathing and nearer than hands or feet ', one with our nature at its highest and at its best.

The *Opus Postumum* then, if I am right, certainly does not suggest that Kant in his last days abandoned his faith in God as a real Being, or that for him Religion merged itself in Philosophy, as it does for example in the system of Croce. He had always believed in God, and thought that faith in him was bound up with the moral life, in the living of which alone man possessed true dignity, because in living it, and only so, did he attain to true personality. The difficulties of theoretically justifying this faith had produced that hesitation in the use of religious language, that meticulous caution in the indulgence of the religious sentiments, which is so apt to strike a certain chill into the readers of his earlier works. But now, at the end of his life, encouraged perhaps by the open immanentism of his younger contemporaries, he was prepared to repudiate more outspokenly the deism which had been so predominant in his youth—the deism which taught a merely transcendent God, whom we had to suppose in order to explain the order of the world, but who was too remote from human concerns to be in any true sense the 'heart and rule of life', and who was to be honoured rather by intellectual acknowledgement than by a strict life of duty. But just because he felt less haunted by this kind of deism, he could now more fully than before recognize in the Moral Law itself, by which his religious emotions had always been most deeply stirred, God and (as he puts it now for the first time) his *Personality* immediately revealed to the soul as the supreme reality, *ens summum, summa intelligentia, summum bonum*.

VII

CONCLUSION

WHAT are we to say finally of Kant's Philosophy of Religion as a whole ?

I would suggest that in certain respects it possesses a value which is by no means merely archaeological, in the sense of interesting us only as a curiosity in the past history of thought. At a period when there is an obvious tendency in many quarters, no doubt by way of reaction from exaggerations in the opposite direction, which the treatment of the matter by Kant may have assisted in fostering, to dwell on the non-rational or at least unrationalized element in religion,—and in particular on its primitive indifference to our moral distinctions—it is of the highest importance to recall to ourselves certain truths which lie at the heart of Kant's thought as exhibited in his *Religion innerhalb der Grenzen der blossen Vernunft* and in his other writings on religion. I shall reckon these as three.

1. The first of these three truths is that of the *implicit rationality of Religion*. It is especially important to call attention to this truth in view of the very favourable reception lately accorded in theological circles in this country to a remarkable work devoted to emphasizing the presence of a *non-rational* element as fundamentally characteristic

of religion. I refer to Professor Rudolf Otto's *Das Heilige*.[1]

I am entirely in agreement with Professor Otto in holding that there is in religious experience a specific element of feeling or emotion, apart from which we have not Religion at all ; and that, for example, all proofs of God's existence from premises of a general character may either be said to establish (so far as they are successful) not the existence of the God of religion, but merely of an ' Absolute ' or ' Supreme Being ', such as we can only construe as the object of religious experience in so far as our processes of argument are secretly motived or interpreted by what we have recognized through the specific emotional response to which I have referred. But this, which is true *mutatis mutandis* of all forms of human experience,—not only of the moral and the aesthetic but even of the geometrical, which can only arise in a being with the specific intuition of space—does not make Religion non-rational or compel us to regard as peculiar to Religion the presence in it of *an* element presupposed in all reasoning about it; although no doubt this element itself is here as elsewhere of a peculiar or specific nature. In clearing our minds upon this subject the study of

[1] Recently translated under the title of *The Idea of the Holy*. I may in passing observe that the translation seems to me, really, though no doubt unintentionally, to underline unnecessarily that emphasis on the non-rational character of a certain element in Religion which is already, to my mind, disproportionate in the original work.

so far as it at all regards human conduct, satisfy the demands of the moral consciousness. Hence the insistence, so characteristic of Kant's philosophy of religion, that any practice which attempts, or any theory which allows it to be possible, to get at God, so to say, behind the back of the Moral Law—or to set side by side with our duties to one another special 'court-duties', as he calls them, to God, which thereupon must inevitably tend to take precedence of the former—is entirely inconsistent with any religion in which an enlightened conscience can acquiesce.

3. Kant's emphasis upon the *ethical* or *ethically rational character of the Christian religion*, as the feature distinctive of it among the religions of the world, entitling it to stand apart from the rest as the true religion, is of the highest importance. It is all the more so as a certain historical situation is apt to make us perhaps relatively less attentive to this aspect of Christianity than it deserves. For it is a note of modern civilization, as compared with ancient and medieval,—and it has become more obvious within the last hundred years than it was in Kant's own day—that the universality of religion and its fundamental importance in human affairs are no longer assumed as a matter of course, as in earlier ages they were wont to be. This does not by any means imply that religion is less influential in the lives of those who profess it than before—rather perhaps the reverse—but that, while once it was taken for granted that men should profess some religion,

and that religious agreement or disagreement constituted a most important bond or division (as the case
might be) between men, of which account must be
taken in all affairs, public or private, Religion now is
by very many people, not all of them by any means
irreligious themselves, to a considerable extent regarded as something, the influence of which, in
determining the public or political connexions of
nations or individuals, it is in accordance with an
enlightened outlook so far as possible to eliminate,
and a regard to which in ordinary social intercourse
cannot be assumed as a matter of course without
a certain indelicacy or impertinence.[1] The result
of this change is that, whereas Christianity was at
first discriminated from rival religions by the com-
parative rationality of its beliefs, the spirituality of
its worship, and the moral elevation of the life which
it required, in modern days, in the presence of a
civilization (largely its own creation) which is scientific in its intellectual habits, and which, if it admits
worship at all, seeks in it rather aesthetic expression
than a magical or quasi-magical control of the environment, and is inclined to find in the promotion
of morality the only generally intelligible justification of religious teaching, Christianity appears to be
discriminated by retaining beliefs in supernatural
occurrences, in the mysterious efficacy of ritual acts,
and in the obligation, over and above ordinary moral
duties, of a kind of behaviour, the value of which is

[1] Cp. my essay on ' The Place of Christianity in Modern Civilization ' in *Essays on Science and Religion.*

only intelligible on a hypothesis not universally or perhaps even generally admitted. Under these circumstances there is a real temptation to Christianity to fall back upon a view essentially pre-Christian, to cherish the thought of a God who requires sacrifice at least as much as mercy, and to identify *religion* with precisely what we cannot assure ourselves is rationally justified or morally necessary, but which, partly for that very reason, excites the feeling—which has the charm of exclusiveness about it—of having to do with something ' quite other ' (*ganz andere* is Otto's phrase) than the world of reciprocal daily duties which we share with all our neighbours alike. Against this dangerous temptation a study of Kant's philosophy of religion may I think serve as a useful safeguard.

Having thus enumerated what seem to be the most valuable features of Kant's teaching on the subject of Religion, I now turn to the two points in which I think we may reasonably find it deficient.

1. As I have several times pointed out Kant's mind like that of the authors of the French Revolution, whose analogue he, with his philosophical revolution, has often been said to be in the world of thought, was profoundly *unhistorical* and *individualistic*. This of course very specially affects his treatment of Religion. For in Science or in Art or even in Morality man is less explicitly conscious than in Religion of his life as *social* and *historical*, laden with past memories and future hopes which he shares with those who are members of the same community. But in Religion

—in Christianity at any rate—he finds himself face to face not with eternal and unchangeable laws or relations, with a beauty which is one with truth—' all we know on earth and all we need to know ',—or even with a categorical imperative, indifferent to whether it ever has been or will be obeyed, but with a *living* God, manifested in an *historical* person and in an *historical* Church.

Now to Kant the moral experience, in which he held Religion to be rooted, and apart from which he acknowledged no experience to be truly religious, although it is an experience of social rights and duties, presents itself in the first place as a command, confronting the individual conscience with an authority which it cannot fail to recognize. The thought of the moral community is reached only indirectly through the recognition of others as equally subject to the law with oneself, and so united by this bond of a common allegiance into a realm of free beings, ends in themselves, for each of which the will expressed in the law is in the last resort his own. In the book on *Religion innerhalb der Grenzen der blossen Vernunft* the Church or Kingdom of God appears not as the natural environment of the religious life, wherein it has its origin and its field of exercise, but rather as a voluntary union designed to counteract the evil effects inevitable in the natural intercourse of men with one another. Nor does Kant discover in History, whether the history of religion or any other, the concrete reality from which the sciences, natural or moral, abstract the laws and principles with which they concern themselves ; it is for him rather a mere illustration of these, and in many cases a very imperfect and unsatisfactory one. Thinking of it thus, he undoubtedly underrates the extent to which religious life is necessarily conditioned by the tradition which carries on its past into its present, and the influence of which is really traceable, even though by himself largely ignored, in his own moral convictions, no less than in the assumption of a transcendent Author of Nature made by earlier thinkers and censured by him in his *Critique of Pure Reason* and elsewhere ; and also underrates the importance to Religion itself of faith in an historical revelation ; although this need not be—indeed cannot properly be at all—faith in past events as such, but rather the consciousness of participation in the memories of a present society, in whose life the individual's religious life is rooted, just as his secular life is rooted in that of his nation.

2. The other feature of Kant's thought which may be criticized as injurious to his full understanding of Religion is one which characterizes his whole system of thought. It is that suggested by the words ' *als ob* '. [1]

This is his view that while, in discovering the structure of the world which confronts it, the mind is discovering its own structure, yet (or rather, therefore) we must never affirm this discovery to hold

[1] His commentator Vaihinger has made these words the designation of his own philosophy ; with which I have, I must confess, no first-hand acquaintance.

good of things as they are *in themselves*. Thus we must explain organic nature *as though* it were due to the design of a Creator, but not assert dogmatically that it is thus due ; and act *as though* there were a God to whom we are responsible, and who orders the world on the principles on which our conscience constrains us to order our conduct ; but again not dogmatically to affirm his existence as a speculative truth. So far as this attitude of Kant's warns us not to confuse different kinds of evidence, or to neglect the fact that certain ideas could only be obtained from certain specific kinds of experience, although, once obtained, they may help us in dealing with other kinds of experience which could never of themselves have suggested them, so far it is a very wholesome discipline of the mind to note and give full weight to his denunciations of ' dogmatism '. But it is not necessary to follow him in making mathematical and physical science the sole standard of genuine knowledge, or in consequence to treat experiences in which the whole of our personality is involved as somehow inferior in validity to the results of abstraction. This is not indeed an entirely fair representation of his thought ; he may be said to have redressed the tendency here indicated by his doctrine of the primacy of the Practical Reason over the Theoretical, a doctrine put forward precisely on the ground that the whole personality is involved in the life of duty as it is not in the departmental activity of scientific investigation. But it points to an element which always held him back from doing full justice to the realism implicit in his idealism; I mean to the possibility of interpreting the doctrine that in knowing Nature we discover the structure of Mind as a recognition that this structure is in fact the structure of Reality itself.

In our study of Kant's philosophy of religion we have thus to make allowance for his unhistorical individualism and for the element of subjectivism which remains in his idealistic theory of knowledge. But although neither of these tendencies are without representatives in the world of philosophical thought to-day, they are neither of them in much favour among those whose sympathy with theology is likely to lead them to occupy themselves with its history. And for such the great work of Kant, of whose contents I have given an inadequate summary, contains teaching all the more valuable that it lays especial stress on considerations somewhat out of fashion among professional scholars.

There are several matters which a full consideration of Kant's Philosophy of Religion could not pass over, but which are not touched upon in this book. Nothing has been said of its immediate literary antecedents nor of its immense influence direct and indirect on subsequent theological thought. But it will have served its purpose if it should succeed in attracting any readers to the careful study of his own work upon the subject, a work to which, I think, one never returns without renewed interest and admiration.

INDEX OF WORKS OF KANT
REFERRED TO IN THIS BOOK

Kritik der praktischen Vernunft, 1788. H. v. 1 foll. B. v. 1 foll.
  pp. 62 foll.
    B. v. 161 ; p. 172 f.
    B. v. 76, 7 ; p. 195.
    B. v. 87 ; p. 195.

Sieben kleine Aufsätze aus den Jahren 1788–91. H. iv. 497 foll.
  [B. xix.]
    H. iv. 505 ; p. 23.

Kritik der Urtheilskraft, 1790. H. v. 171 foll. B. v. 165 foll.
  pp. 69 foll.

Ueber das Misslingen aller philosophischen Versuche in der Theodicee,
  1791. H. vi. 75 foll. B. viii. 255 foll.
    pp. 87 foll.

Die Religion innerhalb der Grenzen der blossen Vernunft, 1793.
  H. vi. 95 foll. B. vi. 1 foll.
    pp. 91 foll.
    B. vi. 195 ; p. 24.

Metaphysische Anfangsgründe der Tugendlehre, 1797. H. vii.
  175 foll. B. vi. 373 foll.
    B. vi. 404, 433 ; p. 59.

Der Streit der Facultäten, 1798. H. vii. 321 foll. B. vii. 1 foll.
    pp. 168 foll.

Briefe. H. viii. 647 foll. B. x–xiii.
    an Mendelssohn (1760), B. x. 69 foll. ; **p. 35.**

Nachlass. H. viii. 607 foll. B. xiv–xxi.
    H. viii. 624 ; p. 173. [B. xix.]

Opus postumum. Ed. Adickes, 1920.
    pp. 178 foll.

GENERAL INDEX